*Salvation Story*

# Salvation Story

A Biblical Commentary on
Human Violence and Godly Peace

David R. Froemming

RESOURCE *Publications* • Eugene, Oregon

SALVATION STORY
A Biblical Commentary on Human Violence and Godly Peace

Copyright © 2016 David R. Froemming. All rights reserved. Except for brief quotations in critical publications or reviews, no part of this book may be reproduced in any manner without prior written permission from the publisher. Write: Permissions, Wipf and Stock Publishers, 199 W. 8th Ave., Suite 3, Eugene, OR 97401.

Resource Publications
An Imprint of Wipf and Stock Publishers
199 W. 8th Ave., Suite 3
Eugene, OR 97401

www.wipfandstock.com

PAPERBACK ISBN: 978-1-5326-0277-1
HARDCOVER ISBN: 978-1-5326-0970-1
EBOOK ISBN: 978-1-5326-0969-5

Manufactured in the U.S.A.                    OCTOBER 18, 2016

Biblical passages and commentary based on a reading of scripture using the mimetic theory of René Girard within the context of evolution.

Scripture quotations throughout are from New Revised Standard Version Bible. Copyright ©1989 National Council of the Churches of Christ in the United States of America. Used by permission. All rights reserved.

# Contents

*Preface* | *vii*

*Acknowledgments* | *xiii*

1 Samuel 8 | 1

Isaiah | 4

Isaiah 11 | 10

Joshua 6 | 12

Exodus 1 | 16

Exodus 3 | 18

Exodus 20 | 20

Exodus 8 and 9 | 22

Deuteronomy 5 | 25

Genesis 39 | 29

Genesis 2 | 32

Luke 1 | 34

Genesis 3 | 36

Leviticus 16 | 40

Numbers 25 | 42

Genesis 1–2 | 45

Daniel 1 | 49

Daniel 9 | 52

## Contents

John 1 | 60
Mark 1 | 63
Romans 6 | 65
Mark 2 | 67
Mark 3 | 70
Luke 5 | 76
Philippians 2 | 79
Mark 6 | 81
Mark 10 | 85
Luke 23 | 90
John 20 | 96
Ephesians | 104
1 Corinthians | 111
Romans 1–2 | 117

*Epilogue* | 126
*Bibliography* | 133

# Preface

HAVING WORKED FULL-TIME IN congregations as a Christian educator for fourteen years and as a pastor ten years, I have observed first-hand the potential for human conflict. Martin Luther's Latin phrase *homo en curvatus*, "humans are curved inward," is all too real, in light of human conflict rooted in the rivalry of in-groups, out-groups, and scapegoats. I have observed the polarization between fundamentalists and atheists. This polarization has produced more heat than light, more rivalry than dialogue, more fragmented thinking than understanding and wisdom. My position is that the bible and evolution need to be placed into conversation, not in opposition to one another, if we are going to be "saved" from our current phase in evolution where we are stuck in rivalry mode. Fundamentalism has managed to reduce the bible to morality at the expense of recreating the very religions of idolatry surrounding the Israelites and Christians. The "salvation story" reveals human violence and the human systems of "goodness" and morality that oppress others and conduct violence in the name of their religion. Meanwhile atheists influenced by such works as James Frazer's *The Golden Bough*, Robert Graves' *The White Goddess* and Joseph Campbell's *The Masks of God*, have relegated the bible to the works of ancient mythology. They neglect attention to the detail of varied genres, biblical languages, and what René Girard and others have observed in the bible, namely that unlike mythology which conceals human violence, the biblical narrative exposes it and ultimately refuses to be part of human rivalry and violence. In fact, Christianity is not a religion but a movement that marks the end of religion as a system that condones and conceals human violence.

By returning the bible to its source and place in our human story, the story of evolution, I hope to give several illustrations that offer to you a renewed perspective of the salvation story that calls us to turn from destruction and live. I draw upon undergraduate and graduate work in religious studies encompassing the Judeo-Christian tradition as well as world religions, women's studies, the biblical languages, and the contributions of those who believe in evolution. I find that René Girard's work on mimetic theory, namely that we learn through imitation yet enter into rivalry with those who are too much like us, takes on great significance within the rise of patriarchal male-dominated culture; the development of the hunt, agriculture, economy, and warfare. Jean Pierre Dupuy observes that even as modern society sheds religion amid technological advances, mimetic violence continues to exist in secular systems of the marketplace, political infrastructures, racism, technology, science, and the military industrial complex. Therefore, a new conversation is needed that re-engages biblical texts for the value they hold in revealing and understanding human violence within our current evolutionary phase of patriarchal culture.

Even if we could erase the bible from human history, the human condition that it is addressing would persist and threaten the future of human life on earth. The rise of patriarchal culture in evolution marks a period of both great scientific and technological innovation and great destructiveness that now threatens to end human life on earth. The bible is both the product of patriarchal culture and the critique of patriarchal culture contained in written accounts of "the salvation story" in multiple oral and literary forms of language that hold the hope of resolving humanity's paradox of power. The biblical tradition evolved amid the mythologies of ancient Mesopotamia yet itself is not merely another patriarchal mythology but a "salvation story" that when read in the context of evolution, decodes myth and religion as human systems that justify and conceal violence, oppression, and victimization. This "salvation story" has evolved and continues to evolve not as one more religion but rather as a rising consciousness transcending the powers of death and systems of cultural violence in order to produce faith in a living God and love for one's neighbor. The bible is the product of evolution and needs to be read in the context of evolution, lest we continue to misinterpret and subvert it into religion and violence.

In his book *The God Delusion*, Richard Dawkins sees the evolution of religion tied to memetic natural selection. Memes are human-made cultural ideas that evolve as they are communicated among people through language, symbols, and rituals. Dawkins finds it plausible that genes and memes are working in natural selection in evolution to create religion, often for the control and manipulation of people.[1] However, noting the work of René Girard, I find that we must not merely look to the memes but also to the human process that is producing them. The human process is found in the Greek biblical word pronounced (*mi-may-tace*), for "imitator." As Paul writes in 1 Corinthians 11:1, "Be imitators of me, as I am of Christ." As humans we learn through imitating the sights and sounds produced by other humans. This process of mimicking creates our social identity and is the very basis of our existence as social beings. It is my claim that the process of mimesis has run into a problem as humans evolved out of the goddess-centered religions into the current male-dominated phase of patriarchy. Namely, as humans shed their creation-centered identity in the symbol of the goddess who represented all of life, fertility, death, re-birth, and gained individual identity, it was done also at the expense of introducing the experience of social alienation. This caused humans to unconsciously use their mimetic skills to gain social approval, thus introducing rivalry and violence, particularly group violence upon those who are not socially approved and who become their scapegoats. Mythology (stories of gods and goddesses, often in conflict and battle) is the memes or ideas constructed to condone and conduct scapegoating for the sake of the social order based on religion. The "salvation story" evolved to

---

1. Dawkins, *The God Delusion*, 191–207.

# Preface

expose religion, reject violence, and give us new identity in Jesus Christ and life beyond scapegoating and death.

My writing takes the form of a biblical commentary so that the reader may have easy access to texts and engage in reading the passage for one's self. Second, texts provide the reader with illustrations of both the copying of violence from other cultures in scripture as well as the transformation of violent myths from other cultures into narratives that are peaceful, life giving, and even humorous. It is the use of mimetic theory in reading these texts which produces "a living Word"—a narrative for understanding our present culture and context. This is my attempt to offer a primer for reading the bible in such a way as to provide an adequate taste of the "living Word" that Douglas John Hall is calling for in his book titled *Waiting for Gospel: An Appeal to the Dispirited Remnants of Protestant Establishment*. Hall writes:

> The Biblicism and biblical literalism of fundamentalism old and new will not be corrected by a modernism that denies the Bible any special pre-eminence, but only by a deeper familiarity with the Spirit that it can in no way contain. The easy division of humankind into saved and unsaved, sheep and goats, good and evil, will not be corrected by silence about evil any more than by sentimentalism that sweeps all distinctions in human behavior under the rug of bourgeois niceness; it will only be changed and deepened by an anthropology that recognizes both the call to obedience and the need for forgiveness even where those ordinarily regarded as 'good' are concerned.[2]

It is my conviction that mimetic theory provides the key to the understanding of our human nature that is being encountered in the bible. The cultural dynamic of centralized power has set in motion human rivalry and violence which we must be "saved from" for human life to continue on this planet. It is my hope that the following readings and commentary speak to the violence, fear, and oppression prevalent in our world, and provide some illustrations

---

2. Hall, *Waiting for Gospel*, 14.

## Preface

as to how biblical texts can nurture in us a living Word and a viable salvation story for our time.

If there is a principal guiding my selection of texts I would say it is the passages of scripture that stand out to me as being lost in the polarity of the present culture. I avoid subheadings for the texts because I do not want to frame the reading of the text in any other way than a sense for the dynamics of mimetic theory. I chose the word "salvation" in my title because fundamentalism has stalled our culture in a senseless debate between evolution and creationism, never getting us out of the first article of the creed—never moving us beyond the issue of creation to the event of salvation. Girard is centered in a reading of scripture from the cross of Jesus Christ—the central drama of our salvation.

# Acknowledgments

THROUGH ENCOUNTERING THE WORK of René Girard I have grown in an understanding and an appreciation as to how the life and example of other people have become part of my own engagement with scripture. By their passion for teaching scripture, its historical/cultural context, its languages, and its relationship to so many other disciplines, I have been nurtured and mentored as an educator and pastor.

I want to acknowledge the following people: Rita Burns, Tom Suriano, Dan DiDomizio, Gary Boelhower, Joan Leonard, Loretta Dornisch, David McCarthy, Fran Leap, James Bailey, Nate Frambach, Ann Fritschel, Norma Cook Everist, David Lull, Shannon Jung, Ray Martin, Craig Nessan, Duane Larson, Elizabeth Leeper, James Nieman, Dan Olson, May Burt Persaud, Winston Persaud, Duane Priebe, Gwen Sayler, Thomas Schattauer, and Bill Weiblin.

Thank you to my wife, Kathy O'Brien Froemming, for her love, perseverance, and patience for being with me on my journey in ministry. Thank you to our daughter, Caitlin, and son, Brian, for conversations, feedback, and encouragement to write.

Thank you to Craig Nessan, James Alison, Duane Larson, and Douglas John Hall for reading my work and providing valuable feedback.

Thank you to George Carlson, my ordaining bishop, who gathered his first call pastors to read Douglas John Hall.

Thank you to the communities of Christ Lutheran Church, Lancaster, Wisconsin, and St. Paul Lutheran Church, Potosi, Wisconsin, who have supported me in my ministry.

## Acknowledgments

I give a special thank you to long-time friends Sam and Arlene Jackson, and Gloria Krueger who have supported my journey in ministry.

Rev David R. Froemming

# 1 Samuel 8

1 When Samuel became old, he made his sons judges over Israel . . . 3 Yet his sons did not follow in his ways, but turned aside after gain; they took bribes and perverted justice. 4 Then all the elders of Israel gathered together and came to Samuel at Ramah, 5 and said to him, "You are old and your sons do not follow in your ways; appoint for us, then, a king to govern us, like other nations." 6 But the thing displeased Samuel when they said, "Give us a king to govern us." Samuel prayed to the LORD 7 and the LORD said to Samuel, "Listen to the voice of the people in all that they say to you; for they have not rejected you, but they have rejected me from being king over them. 8 Just as they have done to me, from the day I brought them up out of Egypt to this day, forsaking me and serving other gods, so also they are doing to you. 9 Now then, listen to their voice; only—you shall solemnly warn them, and show them the ways of the king who shall reign over them." 10 So Samuel reported all the words of the LORD to the people who were asking him for a king. 11 He said, "These will be the ways of the king who will reign over you: he will take your sons and appoint them to his chariots and to be his horsemen, and to run before his chariots; 12 and he will appoint for himself commanders of thousands and commanders of fifties, and some to plow his ground and to reap his harvest, and to make his implements of war and the equipment of his chariots. 13 He will take your daughters to be perfumers and cooks and bakers. 14 He will take the best of your fields and vineyards and olive orchards and give them to his courtiers. 15 He will take one-tenth of your grain and of your vineyards and give it to his officers and his courtiers. 16 He will take your male and female slaves, and the best of your cattle and

donkeys, and put them to his work. 17 He will take one-tenth of your flocks, and you shall be his slaves. 18 And in that day you will cry out because of your king, whom you have chosen for yourselves; but the LORD will not answer you in that day." 19 But the people refused to listen to the voice of Samuel; they said, "No! but we are determined to have a king over us, 20 so that we also may be like other nations, and that our king may govern us and go out before us and fight our battles."

I BEGIN WITH THE above story from 1 Samuel 8 because it illustrates the human nature of copying the actions of one another. No matter what Samuel tells the Israelites concerning the trials and tribulations of having a king, the Israelites want a king "so that they may be like other nations." René Girard refers to this trait in humans with the Greek word *mimesis,* which means "to mimic." Mimesis, copying, is the basis of all life forms, yet even more so in humans.[1] In his book *The Selfish Gene,* Richard Dawkins notes that genes for mimicry are favored in natural selection.[2] Girard states that it is the increase in the ability to imitate one another that led to the development of the brain for *homo sapiens*—humans.[3]

While our human ability to imitate one another is the basis for all of our learning and development, it also contains the root of our conflict, which begins in opposing individuals or parties desiring to imitate the same thing, thus bringing about rivalry. The above reading from Samuel makes this connection as Samuel illustrates how having a king will lead them into wars with their neighbors. The king will make their sons and daughters into slaves, and take their crops and livestock from them (verses 12–17). Samuel has recalled the very events that led the Israelites to being slaves into Egypt, and yet they insist on having a king.

That we copy others makes us radically social beings much more than individuals. All our inventiveness and all our works

---

1. Girard, *Things Hidden Since the Foundation of the World,* 90.
2. Dawkins, *The Selfish Gene,* 32.
3. Girard, *Things Hidden Since the Foundation of the World,* 94.

## 1 Samuel 8

of creative beauty comes through mimesis. Yet at the same time, nothing more than our ability to imitate lends to our being more combative and more violent than all other mammals.[4] In fact the only other species besides humans who conduct warfare and slavery are social insects such as ants.[5] This paradox takes me to a saying from Martin Luther, namely that human beings are simultaneously saints and sinners.[6]

It is my conviction that the stories in the bible reveal the human capacity for violence and that this violence is ultimately not from God, but rather the gods fashioned by the people that are representations (idols) of their own doing. For too long now, the biblical accounts have been mistaken to be just more stories of primitive mythology. René Girard charges this is because *we do not know how to decipher the documents we do possess.*[7] It is by recognizing that biblical texts are a new creative engagement of the human condition's capacity to copy others, and the conflict and violence it causes, that we will find the *story of salvation* which evolves to turn us from our own human self-destruction as a species.

In the following chapters I will work with biblical texts to illustrate the other dynamics that are part of the paradox of human copying—both its violent and creative capacities. In doing so I will be mainly in an exchange between the works of Richard Dawkins and René Girard, along with others, to draw out how the biblical texts are an engagement with the evolutionary condition that we have as humans—copying and mimetic rivalry. The salvation story is designed to reveal human violence, lay bare our human capacity to scapegoat—victimize others, and conceal the evidence. The salvation story engages our human blindness to this violence by offering us identity beyond the need for rivalry, identity in Jesus Christ.

---

4. Girard, *The One by Whom Scandal Comes*, 5.
5. Dawkins, *The Selfish Gene*, 177.
6. Lazareth, *Christians in Society*, 71.
7. Girard, *The Scapegoat*, 25.

# Isaiah

1:1 The vision of Isaiah son of Amoz, which he saw concerning Judah and Jerusalem in the days of Uzziah, Jotham, Ahaz, and Hezekiah, kings of Judah. 2 Hear, O heavens, and listen, O earth; for the LORD has spoken: I reared children and brought them up, but they have rebelled against me. 3 The ox knows its owner, and the donkey its master's crib; but Israel does not know, my people do not understand.

ISAIAH IS A PROPHET at the time of the fall of the northern empire of ancient Israel to the Assyrians in 721 BCE. Isaiah lists off the kings who are part of a monarchy that treats its own people unjustly. Long before Warner Brother Cartoons' character of Bugs Bunny outsmarted Elmer Fudd, Isaiah portrayed the animals as being wiser than humans.[1] Isaiah sees how the power of his own kings now oppresses the people, especially the poor. Isaiah writes, "What do you mean by crushing my people, by grinding the face of the poor? says the Lord GOD of hosts" (Isaiah 3:15). Walter Brueggemann wrote about how the exploits of the kings numb the people and leave them feeling powerless. It is the task of the prophet to engage the people back into the experience of their suffering and death.[2] Isaiah uses nature to do so. In chapter 6, he depicts Israel as a tree finding itself reduced to a stump.

> 6:8 Then I heard the voice of the Lord saying, "Whom shall I send, and who will go for us?" And I said, "Here am I; send me!" 9 And he said, "Go and say to this people: 'Keep listening, but do not comprehend; keep

---

1. The Gospel of Luke thus has Jesus born in a manger with animals, Luke 2:7.

2. Brueggemann, *The Prophetic Imagination*, 46.

> looking, but do not understand.' 10 Make the mind of this people dull, and stop their ears, and shut their eyes, so that they may not look with their eyes, and listen with their ears, and comprehend with their minds, and turn and be healed." 11 Then I said, "How long, O Lord?" And he said: "Until cities lie waste without inhabitant, and houses without people, and the land is utterly desolate; 12 until the LORD sends everyone far away, and vast is the emptiness in the midst of the land. 13 Even if a tenth part remain in it, it will be burned again, like a terebinth or an oak whose stump remains standing when it is felled." The holy seed is its stump.

Isaiah develops a paradox of power whereby the more Israel attempts to listen, it cannot comprehend; the more it tries to look, it cannot see. Isaiah depicts human nature as utterly blind. I find Isaiah's depiction of Israel not at all far removed from Richard Dawkins's claim on evolution, namely that "It has no mind and no mind's eye. It does not plan for the future. It has no vision, for foresight at all. If it can be said to play the role of the watchmaker in nature, it is the *blind* watchmaker."[3]

Isaiah also uses the image of Israel as vineyard in Chapter 5:

> 5:1 Let me sing for my beloved my love-song concerning his vineyard: My beloved had a vineyard on a very fertile hill. 2 He dug it and cleared it of stones, and planted it with choice vines; he built a watchtower in the midst of it, and hewed out a wine vat in it; he expected it to yield grapes, but it yielded wild grapes. 3 And now, inhabitants of Jerusalem and people of Judah, judge between me and my vineyard. 4 What more was there to do for my vineyard that I have not done in it? When I expected it to yield grapes, why did it yield wild grapes?
>
> 5 And now I will tell you what I will do to my vineyard. I will remove its hedge, and it shall be devoured; I will break down its wall, and it shall be trampled down. 6 I will make it a waste; it shall not be pruned or hoed, and it shall be overgrown with briers and thorns; I will also command the clouds that they rain no rain upon it. 7 For

---

3. Dawkins, *The Blind Watchmaker*, 9.

> the vineyard of the LORD of hosts is the house of Israel, and the people of Judah are his pleasant planting; he expected justice, but saw bloodshed; righteousness, but heard a cry! 8 Ah, you who join house to house, who add field to field, until there is room for no one but you, and you are left to live alone in the midst of the land! 9 The LORD of hosts has sworn in my hearing: Surely many houses shall be desolate, large and beautiful houses, without inhabitant. 10 For ten acres of vineyard shall yield but one bath, and a homer of seed shall yield a mere ephah. 11 Ah, you who rise early in the morning in pursuit of strong drink, who linger in the evening to be inflamed by wine, 12 whose feasts consist of lyre and harp, tambourine and flute and wine, but who do not regard the deeds of the LORD, or see the work of his hands! 13 Therefore my people go into exile without knowledge; their nobles are dying of hunger, and their multitude is parched with thirst. 14 Therefore Sheol has enlarged its appetite and opened its mouth beyond measure; the nobility of Jerusalem and her multitude go down, her throng and all who exult in her. 15 People are bowed down, everyone is brought low, and the eyes of the haughty are humbled. 16 But the LORD of hosts is exalted by justice, and the Holy God shows himself holy by righteousness. 17 Then the lambs shall graze as in their pasture, fatlings and kids shall feed among the ruins.

Keeping with his construction of paradox Isaiah writes in 3:14, "The LORD enters into judgment with the elders and princes of his people: It is you who have devoured the vineyard; the spoil of the poor is in your houses." Isaiah depicts Israel as a vineyard that is trampling itself. This makes perfectly good sense in terms of the paradox of human power I noted earlier with *mimesis*—our human capacity to copy—to create yet at the same time also enter into destructive rivalry. René Girard notes, "There is no human society that is not liable to break down as a result of its own violence."[4] In Isaiah's paradox of power, it is not the Lord who is destructive, it is humanity itself.

---

4. Girard, *The One by Whom Scandal Comes*, 31.

## ISAIAH

Verse 15, "People are bowed down, everyone is brought low, and the eyes of the haughty are humbled," parallels both the image of a trampled vineyard (3:14) and a tree that has been reduced to its stump (6:13). In our age of concentrated wealth and power, where unlimited campaign contributions replace actual democracy and the voice of the people, where we find the same powers in denial about climate change, Isaiah's vision of human power is timely, for it reminds us that these powers are self-destructive and cannot sustain their own reign as creation itself enters into the Lord's judgment against humanity.

Isaiah's paradox with nature contains the same theme of the unity of redemption between humanity and creation that is found in the prophet Hosea and in Paul's letter to the Romans.

> Hosea 4:2 Swearing, lying, and murder, and stealing and adultery break out; bloodshed follows bloodshed. 3 Therefore the land mourns, and all who live in it languish; together with the wild animals and the birds of the air, even the fish of the sea are perishing.

> Romans 8:22 We know that the whole creation has been groaning in labor pains until now; 23 and not only the creation, but we ourselves, who have the first fruits of the Spirit, groan inwardly while we wait for adoption, the redemption of our bodies.

Isaiah's unity of humanity and creation in his construct of the Lord's judgment and redemption is what Walter Wink once described as an integral worldview where "soul permeates the universe. God is not just within me, but within everything. The universe is suffused with the divine."[5] Wink refers to this as *panentheism,* "where everything is in God and God in everything."[6] It is this integral worldview that we find in Isaiah that is missing in the dualistic worldview we find today in our culture where the materialistic world of the atheist is in conflict with the spiritualist world of the religious fundamentalist. It is this cultural polarity

---

5. Wink, *The Powers That Be,* 20.
6. Ibid.

and conflict of these worldviews, neither of which is biblical, that is blinding us like ancient Israel. Wink argues that we are the first generations in the history of the world to make a conscious choice between these worldviews.[7] Isaiah 7:14 and 8:18 have a name for this integral worldview—*Immanuel (God-with-Us).*

René Girard notes how the prophet Isaiah, Amos, and Micah all denounce the sacrificial violence that ancient Israel was practicing. These sacrifices only masked the human injustices in their nation.[8] Isaiah writes in chapter 1:

> 11 What to me is the multitude of your sacrifices? says the LORD; I have had enough of burnt offerings of rams and the fat of fed beasts; I do not delight in the blood of bulls, or of lambs, or of goats. 12 When you come to appear before me, who asked this from your hand? Trample my courts no more; 13 bringing offerings is futile; incense is an abomination to me. New moon and Sabbath and calling of convocation—I cannot endure solemn assemblies with iniquity. 14 Your new moons and your appointed festivals my soul hates; they have become a burden to me, I am weary of bearing them.

According to Girard breaking out of the cycle of religious violence is incredibly difficult. We are in a double bind of being copied by one another, and at the same time resentful of those who copy us, for they are competing with us over the same object of desire.[9] Ultimately this crisis of rivalry is released by the group on a victim, or scapegoat. What is fascinating in terms of our reading of Isaiah, the sacrificial victim or scapegoat is done purely on the basis of superstition and has no rational basis.[10] Thus, Isaiah writes in 8:19 "Consult the ghosts and the familiar spirits that chirp and mutter; should not a people consult their gods, the dead on behalf of the living."

---

7. Ibid., 22.
8. Girard, *Violence and the Sacred*, 41.
9. Ibid., 147.
10. Ibid., 96.

ISAIAH

In order to stave off the violence of mimetic rivalry, people need differentiation from one another, so as to not feel threatened by the copying of who they are. Isaiah, continuing his construct of paradox, uses sets of animals that would normally be found as foe and prey in nature, and sets them into an order guided by the Lord's wisdom where there is no destructive violence.

# Isaiah 11

1 A shoot shall come out from the stump of Jesse, and a branch shall grow out of his roots. 2 The spirit of the LORD shall rest on him, the spirit of wisdom and understanding, the spirit of counsel and might, the spirit of knowledge and the fear of the LORD. 3 His delight shall be in the fear of the LORD. He shall not judge by what his eyes see, or decide by what his ears hear; 4 but with righteousness he shall judge the poor, and decide with equity for the meek of the earth; he shall strike the earth with the rod of his mouth, and with the breath of his lips he shall kill the wicked. 5 Righteousness shall be the belt around his waist, and faithfulness the belt around his loins. 6 The wolf shall live with the lamb, the leopard shall lie down with the kid, the calf and the lion and the fatling together, and a little child shall lead them. 7 The cow and the bear shall graze, their young shall lie down together; and the lion shall eat straw like the ox. 8 The nursing child shall play over the hole of the asp, and the weaned child shall put its hand on the adder's den. 9 They will not hurt or destroy on all my holy mountain; for the earth will be full of the knowledge of the LORD as the waters cover the sea.

ISAIAH PORTRAYS UNLIKELY PAIRS of animals for his human listeners to copy, thus resolving the crisis of rivalry that is caused by their being too much alike. By doing so, Isaiah is keeping the state of humility for people, depicting animals as the role model for peaceful living! It is the Spirit of the Lord's wisdom, not mere human appearances, that this peaceful co-existing order is held together. Here social justice toward the poor is practiced. The blindness of human sight and the deafness of human hearing will

## ISAIAH 11

not deter this one who is led by the Lord's Spirit of wisdom. And Isaiah ends with an integral vision of all the earth being full of the knowledge of the Lord.

This is the wisdom of the Lord spoken through the prophet Isaiah. It is part of the story that comes to save us from the self-destruction we are trapped in as humans.

# Joshua 6

1 Now Jericho was shut up inside and out because of the Israelites; no one came out and no one went in. 2 The LORD said to Joshua, "See, I have handed Jericho over to you, along with its king and soldiers. 3 You shall march around the city, all the warriors circling the city once. Thus you shall do for six days, 4 with seven priests bearing seven trumpets of rams' horns before the ark. On the seventh day you shall march around the city seven times, the priests blowing the trumpets. 5 When they make a long blast with the ram's horn, as soon as you hear the sound of the trumpet, then all the people shall shout with a great shout; and the wall of the city will fall down flat, and all the people shall charge straight ahead."

15 On the seventh day they rose early, at dawn, and marched around the city in the same manner seven times. It was only on that day that they marched around the city seven times. 16 And at the seventh time, when the priests had blown the trumpets, Joshua said to the people, "Shout! For the LORD has given you the city. 17 The city and all that is in it shall be devoted to the LORD for destruction. Only Rahab the prostitute and all who are with her in her house shall live because she hid the messengers we sent. 18 As for you, keep away from the things devoted to destruction, so as not to covet and take any of the devoted things and make the camp of Israel an object for destruction, bringing trouble upon it. 19 But all silver and gold, and vessels of bronze and iron, are sacred to the LORD; they shall go into the treasury of the LORD." 20 So the people shouted, and the trumpets were blown. As soon as the people heard the sound of the trumpets, they raised a great shout, and the wall fell down flat; so the people charged straight ahead into the

## Joshua 6

city and captured it. 21 Then they devoted to destruction by the edge of the sword all in the city, both men and women, young and old, oxen, sheep, and donkeys.

The story of how the Lord instructed Joshua to conquer the city of Jericho serves as an example of the Israelites' copying the mythology of the culture around them. In the ancient Canaanite culture, between 1792 and 1750 BCE, there is a similar story written in their Ugaritic language. It is called the Story of Keret. In the Story of Keret, the Canaanite god El instructs Keret to lay siege to the city of Udum. Like Joshua, Keret is instructed by El not to attack the walls, but instead cut the city off for seven days.[1] In Joshua 6, Rehab the prostitute is spared. In the Story of Keret, a maiden is spared for Keret.[2] One of the names for God used in the Hebrew Scriptures—*Elohim*—is constructed off of the Canaanite god's name, El.

In his book titled *Laying Down the Sword: Why We Can't Ignore the Bible's Violent Verses,* Philip Jenkins reports that "no actual city of Jericho stood at the time of the conquest . . . Putting the archeological evidence together, Joshua's conquest is close to invisible."[3] So what we have in Joshua 6 is indeed the Israelites' copying of their neighbors' mythology in order to be like them. This presents us with the problem of relegating all the writing of the bible to mythology, which authors such as James Frazer in his work *The Golden Bough,* have done. And works such as Frazer's have led atheists such as Richard Dawkins to buy into this view.[4] I argue that copying is taking place by the Israelites, and yet this copying that tries to conceal and hide real human violence is uncovered in the ongoing story of salvation, and ultimately rejected.

The Story of Joshua, like the Story of Keret, can be likened to our own violent movies and battle games being marketed today during each NFL football game. X-box One games like *Assassins*

---

1. Matthews and Benjamin, *Old Testament Parallels*, 201–5.
2. Ibid., 204.
3. Jenkins, *Laying Down the Sword*, 54–57.
4. Dawkins, *The God Delusion*, 188.

and *Game of War* are not literal events, yet they provide a narrative, in a story that leads us to believe human violence is justifiable and acceptable. In the meantime, real killing and violence is part of our culture. We pass laws for people to conceal and carry guns. Military drones are killing real people in the Middle East. Terrorists are killing real people. Politicians want to take us to war again. And it appears we are living in an endless cycle of human violence.

We need to see the accounts of violence in the Hebrew Bible as evidence of the copying of the Israelites of their neighbor's gods (and goddesses). This copying reveals that they do not understand who their god is at these times. Often the Israelites recreate their own version of what Bernard F. Batto has named "The Combat Myth."[5] And rather than allow texts such as Joshua 6 to be read as approval of violence by God, we need to read them as illustrations that show how the Israelites were mistaken about who God is through the copying of combat myths. Our reading them as literal stories of prescribed living rather than descriptions of mimesis *perpetuates our own human violence.*

Walter Wink says that we must reject what he calls "the myth of redemptive violence," namely that by using violence we can bring an end to violence.[6] Wink is correct; no amount of violence is going to change the underlying human condition of *mimesis*, copying, and the rivalry and conflict that are by-products of it. At the same time, we need to learn what is going on with the copying of these myths in the bible. Richard Dawkins thinks that religion is a kind of "misfiring" in evolution and calls it a "meme"—an idea we carry, like genes, but a meme that is more harmful to us like a "virus."[7] By arguing his case with fundamentalists who read these stories literally, Dawkins is pulled off the mark of his real expertise on evolution, and these myths function as they do, to blind us, and hide the human condition that is rooted in all life in evolution—*mimesis, the process of copying,* not memes. By following Girard's lens of *mimesis* and human rivalry we can view violence in the

---

5. Batto, *Slaying the Dragon*, 168–9.
6. Wink, *The Powers That Be*, 42–48.
7. Dawkins, *The God Delusion*, 186–90.

## Joshua 6

bible as part of the evolving understanding of God who in the culmination of the salvation story rejects all our combat myths.

# Exodus 1

15 The king of Egypt said to the Hebrew midwives, one of whom was named Shiphrah and the other Puah, 16 "When you act as midwives to the Hebrew women, and see them on the birthstool, if it is a boy, kill him; but if it is a girl, she shall live." 17 But the midwives feared God; they did not do as the king of Egypt commanded them, but they let the boys live. 18 So the king of Egypt summoned the midwives and said to them, "Why have you done this, and allowed the boys to live?" 19 The midwives said to Pharaoh, "Because the Hebrew women are not like the Egyptian women; for they are vigorous and give birth before the midwife comes to them." 20 So God dealt well with the midwives; and the people multiplied and became very strong. 21 And because the midwives feared God, he gave them families. 22 Then Pharaoh commanded all his people, "Every boy that is born to the Hebrews you shall throw into the Nile, but you shall let every girl live."

WALTER BRUEGGEMANN OBSERVES THAT the genocide of Egypt by its ruler Pharaoh is rooted in the power of monopoly that at the same time lives in constant fear and anxiety that the many people whom they deprive through their hording will rise up and destroy them. And thus paradoxically their power starts to destroy the very source of their empire, namely the slaves![1] Here we observe what we saw in Isaiah, ultimately in the desire to possess things we become blind to how our own power turns back upon us.

The *myth*, the story the empire uses, is rooted in *scarcity*. Myth functions to conceal how human power is lying to justify its violence and death. Scarcity is a lie. Pharaoh and Egypt have plenty

1. Brueggemann, *Journey to the Common Good*, 9–11.

## Exodus 1

of grain for all to live. Yet, in their rivalry with other empires they cannot get enough grain and thus perpetuate the myth of scarcity. The biblical story, the salvation story, is exposing the lie contained in myth—the human suffering and death behind it.

Today it is not national powers alone that use the myth of scarcity to enslave people and justify genocide; it is global multinational corporate power as well. Today we find ourselves engaged in wars created by privatized multinational corporate power, our national budget drained by Pentagon business contractors, and the debt from the war is used to give the political message of scarcity, which in turn is used to justify the removal of social programs such as health and education. The end goal is global corporations taking over nations through the privatization of all services and replacing government with corporate control of the people and the earth's resources.[2] In the meantime we are kept distracted, indeed blinded, by the threat of terrorism, which uses national security as myth to perpetuate the ongoing violence, keeping the cycle of war debt and privatization going. Like Pharaoh killing his slaves, global corporations are destroying their own consumers, the environment beneath their feet and all around their mansions.

Paul Ricœur has noted that myth is never about morality, it is always about human death and human desire for immortality.[3] Therefore the bible is not a morality book. The bible is an engagement with human myths that conceal violence and death, which in its evolution, sets out to expose human violence and injustice. Yet, this process is no quick matter. For myths also evolve and appear again in yet another form, always in an attempt to hide the violence that is rooted in our human rivalry—mimesis—our copying.

---

2. Klein, *The Shock Doctrine*, 354–407.
3. Ricœur, *The Symbolism of Evil*, 187.

# Exodus 3

1 Moses was keeping the flock of his father-in-law Jethro, the priest of Midian; he led his flock beyond the wilderness, and came to Horeb, the mountain of God. 2 There the angel of the LORD appeared to him in a flame of fire out of a bush; he looked, and the bush was blazing, yet it was not consumed. 3 Then Moses said, "I must turn aside and look at this great sight, and see why the bush is not burned up." 4 When the LORD saw that he had turned aside to see, God called to him out of the bush, "Moses, Moses!" And he said, "Here I am." 5 Then he said, "Come no closer! Remove the sandals from your feet, for the place on which you are standing is holy ground." 6 He said further, "I am the God of your father, the God of Abraham, the God of Isaac, and the God of Jacob." And Moses hid his face, for he was afraid to look at God. 7 Then the LORD said, "I have observed the misery of my people who are in Egypt; I have heard their cry on account of their taskmasters. Indeed, I know their sufferings, 8 and I have come down to deliver them from the Egyptians, and to bring them up out of that land to a good and broad land, a land flowing with milk and honey, to the country of the Canaanites, the Hittites, the Amorites, the Perizzites, the Hivites, and the Jebusites. 9 The cry of the Israelites has now come to me; I have also seen how the Egyptians oppress them. 10 So come, I will send you to Pharaoh to bring my people, the Israelites, out of Egypt." 11 But Moses said to God, "Who am I that I should go to Pharaoh, and bring the Israelites out of Egypt?" 12 He said, "I will be with you; and this shall be the sign for you that it is I who sent you: when you have brought the people out of Egypt, you shall worship God on this mountain." 13 But Moses said to God, "If I come to the Israelites and say to them, 'The God of your

## Exodus 3

ancestors has sent me to you,' and they ask me, 'What is his name?' what shall I say to them?" 14 God said to Moses, "I AM WHO I AM." He said further, "Thus you shall say to the Israelites, 'I AM has sent me to you.'"

MOSES ENCOUNTERS A GOD whose name in Hebrew is *Eheyeh Asher Eheyeh*. *Eheyeh* is the first person of the imperfect tense of the Hebrew verb "to be."[1] The translation really is more like "I am becoming that which is becoming." God is not finalized like something that was made, but rather a living process—"a becoming." Only completed things have names. This living God cannot have a name. Idols have names.[2]

This nameless God of becoming is akin to the meaning of *word*, *"debar"* in Hebrew, which is "event—happening." Thus in Moses' encounter with God we discover a process that is taking place to engage myth, the story of human power that is created by humans, a thing, an idol. God's Word, God's event is now encountering the power of Pharaoh. The *salvation story* in the Old Testament is the emergence of this nameless God who starts to shatter the power of human myth and the oppression and violence behind it.

This is why in Hebrew tradition the name for God is not spoken and the Hebrew word *Adonai (my Lord)* is used. It was not easy for the Israelites to keep straight their nameless God from the idols all around them. And this nameless God is not kept straight from the many idols of powers today by biblical literalists. This nameless God is much more akin to evolution, which we can behold, but not control, through our human power, nor be masters over it. Richard Dawkins, though a great writer on evolution, did not make this distinction, and as a result engaged biblical literalists in an entire book titled *The God Delusion*.[3] In the end neither Dawkins nor the biblical literalists grasp the emergence of this event—this nameless God who is the liberation from our violence, who is not the power of idols and human myths.

1. Fromm, *You Shall Be As Gods*, 26.
2. Ibid., 27.
3. Dawkins, *The God Delusion*.

# Exodus 20

> 4 You shall not make for yourself an idol, whether in the form of anything that is in heaven above, or that is on the earth beneath, or that is in the water under the earth.

ERIC FROMM ARGUES THAT moving from idols to the nameless God of becoming is our being moved from alienation of our self into freedom. It marks an evolution from gods that are material or human to the presence of being engaged in justice, love, and forgiveness. Idols also often represent the authoritarian leaders we cling to out of fear and anxiety. The God that is becoming empowers us to be free from the slavery of idolatry and the power of fear.[1]

Working in close conjunction with Fromm, Paul Tillich sees much of religion as a place of escape from fear and anxiety. Tillich argues that the presence of God is the presence of "the courage to be" despite the threat of non-being and death.[2] It is my wager that it is our human mimetic rivalry over objects that is tied in with the creation of our idols of power, our fearful obedience to their authoritarian power, and the violence and death that this produces. The biblical salvation story is the encounter with a God who is the source of our courage to live for others, life, and world. This courage is indeed *faith*, no longer the blind power of human rivalry, but the ability to love, forgive, and stand for social justice.

Fromm concludes that the problem with *idolatry* is that all our self goes into things, instead of into other people. The self that is free from the idols of power and anxiety, the self that is sane, is the self that is set free from conformity to fear and can now

---

1. Fromm, *You Shall be as Gods*, 17–51.
2. Tillich, *The Courage to Be*, 49–89.

love others.[3] It is this God that is being revealed to Moses in the burning bush. It is this God that frees the Israelites from slavery in Pharaoh's Egypt. Like the God we find in the prophet Isaiah, this God in the book of Exodus "who is becoming" is found in the powers of nature.

---

3. Fromm, *The Sane Society*, 112–84.

# Exodus 8 and 9

1 Then the LORD said to Moses, "Go to Pharaoh and say to him, 'Thus says the LORD: Let my people go, so that they may worship me. 2 If you refuse to let them go, I will plague your whole country with frogs. 3 The river shall swarm with frogs; they shall come up into your palace, into your bedchamber and your bed, and into the houses of your officials and of your people, and into your ovens and your kneading bowls. 4 The frogs shall come up on you and on your people and on all your officials.'"

16 Then the LORD said to Moses, "Say to Aaron, 'Stretch out your staff and strike the dust of the earth, so that it may become gnats throughout the whole land of Egypt.'" 17 And they did so; Aaron stretched out his hand with his staff and struck the dust of the earth, and gnats came on humans and animals alike; all the dust of the earth turned into gnats throughout the whole land of Egypt.

Exodus 9:24 there was hail with fire flashing continually in the midst of it, such heavy hail as had never fallen in all the land of Egypt since it became a nation. 25 The hail struck down everything that was in the open field throughout all the land of Egypt, both human and animal; the hail also struck down all the plants of the field, and shattered every tree in the field.

EXODUS LISTS NINE NATURE plagues in all, and then concludes with a tenth plague that copies the violence done to the Hebrews at the start of this story—the death of the firstborn, only now among the Egyptians. In between the ninth and tenth plagues is the celebration of Passover, a ritual meal in Chapter 12, so that the Israelites may always remember their slavery and the God who led them

## Exodus 8 and 9

to freedom. Then the drama concludes with one more attempt by Pharaoh to destroy the Hebrews as they leave. Again nature, the water of the Red Sea, swallows Pharaoh's army.

This same theme of nature keeping the ever expanding power of humans in check was already used in Genesis 7—the story of the great flood and Noah. Here again, it was the wicked warrior heroes whom God did away with through a great flood—Chapter 6. Paul Ricœur has made the observation that while other neighbors of the Israelites had flood stories, the flood stories of the Israelites differed in one very significant way. Ricœur observes that in primitive myths such as the Babylonian's *Enuma elish* human violence is due to humans copying the violent powers they find in nature.[1] This confirms Girard's observation that behind the gods in the warrior myths are real human victims of violence.[2] However, Ricœur notes that in the biblical flood accounts, it is human violence that initiates the response of nature. Human violence is exposed in the story as being responsible for nature's response.[3]

Think of the climate change debate today. As it turns out, the biblical salvation story holds humans accountable for nature's response. As argued earlier by Walter Wink, the biblical worldview is integral, where humans are tied in with nature and evolution. Humanity cannot claim to be outside of the loop of what is happening in nature. To argue as such is to take the position of primitive pagan religions and abandon the worldview of the bible! The biblical worldview is much more akin to evolution than it is to pagan mythology. On this point the work of Richard Dawkins on the dynamics of evolution is well worth our observation. In his book *The Selfish Gene,* Dawkins observes that ultimately evolution does not reward those who constantly cheat and abuse power. Rather, in evolution cooperation and mutual assistance is the larger strategy for the continuation of life.[4]

---

1. Ricœur, *The Symbolism of Evil*, 175–217.
2. Girard, *The Scapegoat*, 48–49.
3. Ricœur, *The Symbolism of Evil*, 175–217.
4. Dawkins, *The Selfish Gene*, 202–33.

Returning to the *salvation story,* the Israelites once set free will regress to their idols after leaving Egypt. And today we regress in our religious life as we fashion gods in our own images of power, and in our own images of conformity to unjust powers that have once again blinded us through rivalry—our in-groups and out-groups, those we copy, and those we resent for not conforming to our copying. Law alone and law telling us not to make idols is only part of the salvation story's response to the problem of human mimesis. The prophets, as we have already seen in Isaiah, take up the problem of idolatry again, and as we shall see, point us to the other part of the equation—receiving *a new identity* from the God who is becoming.

# Deuteronomy 5

1 Moses convened all Israel, and said to them: Hear, O Israel, the statutes and ordinances that I am addressing to you today; you shall learn them and observe them diligently. 2 The LORD our God made a covenant with us at Horeb. 3 Not with our ancestors did the LORD make this covenant, but with us, who are all of us here alive today. 4 The LORD spoke with you face to face at the mountain, out of the fire. 5 (At that time I was standing between the LORD and you to declare to you the words of the LORD; for you were afraid because of the fire and did not go up the mountain.) And he said: 6 I am the LORD your God, who brought you out of the land of Egypt, out of the house of slavery; 7 you shall have no other gods before me. 8 You shall not make for yourself an idol, whether in the form of anything that is in heaven above, or that is on the earth beneath, or that is in the water under the earth. 9 You shall not bow down to them or worship them; for I the LORD your God am a jealous God, punishing children for the iniquity of parents, to the third and fourth generation of those who reject me, 10 but showing steadfast love to the thousandth generation of those who love me and keep my commandments.

IF BOOKS OF THE bible were movies, Exodus could be titled *Moses One*. Deuteronomy could be titled *Moses Two*. The reason the commandments are given once again is because refugees from the fall of the Northern Kingdom of Israel to the Assyrians in 721 BCE are now coming south to settle into the remaining Southern Kingdom of Judah. Moses is long gone. But the story needs to be retold once again to a new generation of people. The first three verses of Chapter 6 are a recasting of the Israelites' first entrance into the Promised Land for this new generation of refugees:

> 6:1 Now this is the commandment—the statutes and the ordinances—that the LORD your God charged me to teach you to observe in the land that you are about to cross into and occupy, 2 so that you and your children and your children's children may fear the LORD your God all the days of your life, and keep all his decrees and his commandments that I am commanding you, so that your days may be long. 3 Hear therefore, O Israel, and observe them diligently, so that it may go well with you, and so that you may multiply greatly in a land flowing with milk and honey, as the LORD, the God of your ancestors, has promised you.

I am lifting up these texts to show how the work of the reformers who write Deuteronomy are essentially dealing with the same problem of idolatry as earlier writers and that their editing of books at this time reveals that the Israelites were not a monotheistic religion in the united kingdom of Israel and Judah, nor even in Judah. It is not until after the fall of the Southern Kingdom in 587 BCE to the Babylonians that we begin to see the rise of monotheism and the belief in just one God. In his book *The Hebrew Goddess,* Raphael Patai tells how the Hebrew people could not abandon the Canaanite goddess Asherah, who was originally the consort of the Canaanite god El. Instead, the Israelites made Asherah the consort of Yahweh.[1]

The goddess Asherah was connected to the belief that human sex and fertility were related to the fertility of the land. Thus the people engaged in sexual ritual practices and believed the practices had a bearing on the success of their produce from the land and trees. The reformers of Deuteronomy try to denounce the ritual practices centered around the goddess Asherah, but to no avail. Here is some of their editing in the books of 1 Kings and Isaiah, where they have inserted their condemning of Asherah. Here the

---

1. Patai, *The Hebrew Goddess,* 10–41.

translation is "pole," but it is Asherah, a pole-like figurine of the fertility goddess.

> 1 Kings 14:23 For they also built for themselves high places, pillars, and sacred *poles* on every high hill and under every green tree;

> Isaiah 17:8 they will not have regard for the altars, the work of their hands, and they will not look to what their own fingers have made, either the sacred *poles* or the altars of incense.

> Isaiah 27:9 Therefore by this the guilt of Jacob will be expiated, and this will be the full fruit of the removal of his sin: when he makes all the stones of the altars like chalkstones crushed to pieces, no sacred *poles* or incense altars will remain standing.

The reformers from the era of Deuteronomy reveal how religion and culture are intertwined and cannot be separated. Karen Armstrong makes this argument in her book titled *Fields of Blood: Religion and the History of Violence*. Armstrong argues that warfare was indispensable to the ruling class of all agrarian civilizations.[2] Likewise, goddess worship was indispensable to agriculture. Thus we see in the biblical world that the copying of culture and ritual practice is stronger than any religious prohibitions. Sexual fertility rites centered on the goddess Asherah persisted among the Israelites all the way up to the Babylonian exile in 587 BCE, where we find the prophet Jeremiah still taking up the issue.

> Jeremiah 17:2 while their children remember their altars and their sacred *poles*, beside every green tree, and on the high hills,

It is a modern day misperception and misrepresentation of the bible that it is a morality book. For if it is, it failed miserably! I would argue that the violence and sex we see practiced in the bible are essentially religion/culture. And I agree with Rene Girard's

---

2. Armstrong, *Fields of Blood*, 15.

disciple Jean-Pierre Dupuy that what emerges in the God of scripture and Jesus Christ is essentially not *religion*, but rather "the end of religions."[3] Dupuy argues that Christianity is not a morality, but rather an epistemology that is revealing to us the source of our violence and striving to deprive it of its power over us.[4]

Dupuy points out how the power of human mimetic rivalry threatens our existence in such secular realms as economics, technology, nuclear deterrence, the electoral process, and genetic engineering. The ongoing polarized argument between religion and evolution has blinded us from seeing the human problem of mimesis beneath it all. The salvation story is not a morality lesson. The salvation story is the dynamic interplay between scripture and culture where both demand our interpretive skills and in doing so work upon us to uncover the game of human rivalry and violence so that we may live and not perish. Richard Dawkins is right about natural selection and evolution having no design and being blind.[5] Yet Dupuy would add, "The future may have no need of us, but we very much need the future for it is what gives meaning to everything we do."[6]

The reformers of Deuteronomy give us a lesson in how moral claims have no power over the human rivalry within culture and religion. Something is needed beyond law and commandment to deliver our humanity from its violence. I maintain that it is the story, the creative living Word that transforms the vision of who we are in the eyes of a God who is becoming—a God who can transform our tragedy into life and, yes, even laughter.

---

3. Dupuy, *The Mark of the Sacred*, 93.
4. Ibid., 124.
5. Dawkins, *The Blind Watchmaker*, 9.
6. Dupuy, *The Mark of the Sacred*, 63.

# Genesis 39

6 So he left all that he had in Joseph's charge; and, with him there, he had no concern for anything but the food that he ate. Now Joseph was handsome and good-looking. 7 And after a time his master's wife cast her eyes on Joseph and said, "Lie with me." 8 But he refused and said to his master's wife, "Look, with me here, my master has no concern about anything in the house, and he has put everything that he has in my hand. 9 He is not greater in this house than I am, nor has he kept back anything from me except yourself, because you are his wife. How then could I do this great wickedness, and sin against God?" 10 And although she spoke to Joseph day after day, he would not consent to lie beside her or to be with her. 11 One day, however, when he went into the house to do his work, and while no one else was in the house, 12 she caught hold of his garment, saying, "Lie with me!" But he left his garment in her hand, and fled and ran outside. 13 When she saw that he had left his garment in her hand and had fled outside, 14 she called out to the members of her household and said to them, "See, my husband has brought among us a Hebrew to insult us! He came in to me to lie with me, and I cried out with a loud voice; 15 and when he heard me raise my voice and cry out, he left his garment beside me, and fled outside." 16 Then she kept his garment by her until his master came home.

THE STORY OF JOSEPH in Potiphar's house represents the transformation of violent tragic Egyptian mythology into Hebrew comedy. Joseph was hated by his brothers on account of his dream telling and the robe his mother made especially for him (Genesis 37:1–8). His brothers sold him into slavery. They took Joseph's robe, put animal blood on it, and told their father that a wild animal devoured him (Genesis 37:12–36). The above passage is where the story turns into comedy.

The story of Joseph has its parallel in the Egyptian story of two brothers, Anubis and Bata. Like the story of Joseph at the house of his owner, Potiphar, the story of Anubis and Bata contains the sexual advances of a wife toward another man. In the story of Joseph, it is the wife of his master who makes the advances. In the story of Anubis and Bata, it is the wife of Anubis who makes advances at her brother-in-law Bata.

Anubis and Bata are planting grain. Running out of grain, Bata returns home for more seed. He is met by the wife of Anubis who tries to seduce him and have sex with him. Bata is outraged at the idea of having sex with his brother's wife, and departs. The wife of Anubis feels remorse and tries, unsuccessfully, to poison herself to death. Bata tells Anubis of the ordeal, and Anubis tries to kill him. Bata flees and cuts off his penis. Anubis returns home to murder his wife. End of story.[1]

In the story of Joseph at Potiphar's house, the original Hebrew language is loaded with word-play. The word "hand" *yad* in Hebrew can also be translated as "penis." The word for "care," *yada* in Hebrew, also means to know another sexually. Joseph imagines that he has authority over the household granted to him by his owner, Potiphar. In reality, it is Potiphar's wife who speaks the commands for sex, and has "the upper hand," over Joseph's claim to power.

In verse 9, Joseph makes the claim of his obedience to God. Note, "this great evil" is not merely sex, but in the myth it is transforming sin as death that comes out of sexual rivalry. Nonetheless, Potiphar's wife is relentless in her pursuit of Joseph. The use of the Hebrew language in her command "Lie with me!" takes on different nuances each time as to suggest variations of physical sexual engagement. Finally, when no other servants are in the house, Potiphar's wife seizes Joseph's robe (as once did his brothers), and commands him "Lie with me!" Joseph runs outside naked.

---

1. Matthews and Benjamin, *Old Testament Parallels*, 41–45.

## Genesis 39

Joseph's robe has this amazing quality about it—those who hold it tell "lies" (pun intended) about Joseph. Potiphar's wife tells her servants that Joseph was trying to seduce her. The punch line is "See! He (Potiphar) brought in to us a Hebrew man to play around with us." How does she know Joseph is a Hebrew? Joseph's penis is circumcised. Circumcision is the sign of God's covenant with the Israelites (Genesis 17:9–14). Potiphar's wife is left with Joseph's robe in her "hand" looking at Joseph's penis in contempt, suggesting he would be sexual with all the servants of the household. But, she gets no reaction from the servants.

In the end, no one gets mutilated or killed.

In what seems like the original episode of *Desperate Housewives*, Joseph will not be made into the sex-slave of his master's wife. At the same time, Joseph has nowhere near the authority he imagines that he has received from his master. Only Joseph's obedience to his God is what can avert the Anubis and Bata myth's fate of sex and violence. It is brilliant comedy. As I have said more than once from my pulpit, there is a reason why many of America's greatest comedians are Jewish. The Hebrew writers of the salvation story were masters of word-play. The God who is becoming loves to turn our human tragedy into laughter and life.

# Genesis 2

15 The LORD God took the man and put him in the Garden of Eden to till it and keep it. 16 And the LORD God commanded the man, "You may freely eat of every tree of the garden; 17 but of the tree of the knowledge of good and evil you shall not eat, for in the day that you eat of it you shall die." 18 Then the LORD God said, "It is not good that the man should be alone; I will make him a helper as his partner." 19 So out of the ground the LORD God formed every animal of the field and every bird of the air, and brought them to the man to see what he would call them; and whatever the man called every living creature, that was its name. 20 The man gave names to all cattle, and to the birds of the air, and to every animal of the field; but for the man there was not found a helper as his partner. 21 So the LORD God caused a deep sleep to fall upon the man, and he slept; then he took one of his ribs and closed up its place with flesh. 22 And the rib that the LORD God had taken from the man he made into a woman and brought her to the man. 23 Then the man said, "This at last is bone of my bones and flesh of my flesh; this one shall be called Woman, for out of Man this one was taken."

GENESIS CHAPTER TWO IS the earlier creation account, whereas the account given in chapter one is written following the Babylonian exile ending in approximately 500 BCE. I am looking at Genesis 2 in order to note that this creation story reverses the understanding of human life found in previously existing goddess cultures prior to the rise of patriarchal male-centered culture. In her work titled *Gods and Goddesses of Old Europe,* Marija Gimbutas shows the archeological evidence of goddess-centered cultures in the Neolithic

## Genesis 2

period of 7000 to 3500 BCE. Pottery, carvings, and sculptural art from this period reveal that woman was the central source of all human life.[1] According to Gimbutas there were three waves of invasions of patriarchal tribes coming out of present-day Russia who disrupted the Neolithic culture. These waves occurred in 4300 to 4200 BCE, 3400 to 3200 BCE, and 3000 to 2800 BCE.[2] The Hebrew people are a peripheral group within these invasions of male-dominated culture. The rise of patriarchal culture represents the move away from previous vegetarian gathering-based culture to that of the hunt, the rise of animal husbandry, agriculture, and a social system based on power and aggression.[3] Genesis 2 represents the reversal of life coming from woman; now woman is created from man as a rib is taken from his side while he sleeps (verses 21–22).

René Girard makes the case that what people are doing is mostly reading the New Testament from the perspective of the Old. When we do this we read the violence of the culture that is within the Hebrew Bible through the entire body of scripture.[4] Let us note that if we read about the birth of Jesus in Luke's Gospel, we discover that the patriarchal human power has been written out of the equation of who Jesus is, for no human man is part of Mary's pregnancy. This is not a biological claim, but a *theological* claim, that Jesus does not represent the violent power of patriarchal culture.

---

1. Gimbutas, *The Gods and Goddesses of Old Europe*, 17–18.
2. Eisler, *The Chalice and the Blade*, 44.
3. Fromm, *The Anatomy of Human Destructiveness*, 120–75.
4. Girard, *Things Hidden Since the Foundation of the World*, 182–262.

# Luke 1

26 In the sixth month the angel Gabriel was sent by God to a town in Galilee called Nazareth, 27 to a virgin engaged to a man whose name was Joseph, of the house of David. The virgin's name was Mary. 28 And he came to her and said, "Greetings, favored one! The Lord is with you." 29 But she was much perplexed by his words and pondered what sort of greeting this might be. 30 The angel said to her, "Do not be afraid, Mary, for you have found favor with God. 31 And now, you will conceive in your womb and bear a son, and you will name him Jesus. 32 He will be great, and will be called the Son of the Most High, and the Lord God will give to him the throne of his ancestor David. 33 He will reign over the house of Jacob forever, and of his kingdom there will be no end." 34 Mary said to the angel, "How can this be, since I am a virgin?" 35 The angel said to her, "The Holy Spirit will come upon you, and the power of the Most High will overshadow you; therefore the child to be born will be holy; he will be called Son of God. 36 And now, your relative Elizabeth in her old age has also conceived a son; and this is the sixth month for her who was said to be barren. 37 For nothing will be impossible with God."

ELIZABETH SCHÜSSLER FIORENZA NOTES that in the earliest Gospel, Mark, Jesus is referred to as "the son of Mary" (Mark 6:3). According to Fiorenza this is to communicate that Mary was set apart from the power of men.[1] And thus we find in Luke's Gospel the portrayal of Mary as bringing forth the life of God who opposes the powers of the oppressive and the rich—the powers of patriarchal culture.

1. Fiorenza, *Jesus*, 185–6.

## Luke 1

46 And Mary said, "My soul magnifies the Lord, 47 and my spirit rejoices in God my Savior, 48 for he has looked with favor on the lowliness of his servant. Surely, from now on all generations will call me blessed; 49 for the Mighty One has done great things for me, and holy is his name. 50 His mercy is for those who fear him from generation to generation. 51 He has shown strength with his arm; he has scattered the proud in the thoughts of their hearts. 52 He has brought down the powerful from their thrones, and lifted up the lowly; 53 he has filled the hungry with good things, and sent the rich away empty.

It is by reading the scripture from the perspective of Jesus Christ that we bring to light the violent primitive myths and the religion it has left behind. It is the sacrificial reading of scripture by both atheists and fundamentalists that has blinded us from seeing the human violence rooted in *mimesis*. In his book *The God Delusion*, Richard Dawkins claims it is "the memetic"—the evolutionary selection of ideas that has kept religion around, while he himself concludes is quite useless.[2] Dawkins confuses his better work on genes and memes with the human process of *mimesis*—the copying of entire stories, myths that make up culture and religion. In Luke's Gospel we see the entire reversal of the myth of patriarchal culture as the foundation for human existence. The salvation story is not in conflict with evolution. The salvation story liberates us from the violence of human myth and religion.

2. Dawkins, *The God Delusion*, 179–201.

# Genesis 3

1 Now the serpent was more crafty than any other wild animal that the LORD God had made. He said to the woman, "Did God say, 'You shall not eat from any tree in the garden'?" 2 The woman said to the serpent, "We may eat of the fruit of the trees in the garden; 3 but God said, 'You shall not eat of the fruit of the tree that is in the middle of the garden, nor shall you touch it, or you shall die.'" 4 But the serpent said to the woman, "You will not die; 5 for God knows that when you eat of it your eyes will be opened, and you will be like God, knowing good and evil." 6 So when the woman saw that the tree was good for food, and that it was a delight to the eyes, and that the tree was to be desired to make one wise, she took of its fruit and ate; and she also gave some to her husband, who was with her, and he ate. 7 Then the eyes of both were opened, and they knew that they were naked; and they sewed fig leaves together and made loincloths for themselves. 8 They heard the sound of the LORD God walking in the garden at the time of the evening breeze, and the man and his wife hid themselves from the presence of the LORD God among the trees of the garden. 9 But the LORD God called to the man, and said to him, "Where are you?" 10 He said, "I heard the sound of you in the garden, and I was afraid, because I was naked; and I hid myself." 11 He said, "Who told you that you were naked? Have you eaten from the tree of which I commanded you not to eat?" 12 The man said, "The woman whom you gave to be with me, she gave me fruit from the tree, and I ate." 13 Then the LORD God said to the woman, "What is this that you have done?" The woman said, "The serpent tricked me, and I ate." 14 The LORD God said to the serpent, "Because you have done this, cursed are you among all animals and among all wild creatures;

# Genesis 3

upon your belly you shall go, and dust you shall eat all the days of your life. 15 I will put enmity between you and the woman, and between your offspring and hers; he will strike your head, and you will strike his heel." 16 To the woman he said, "I will greatly increase your pangs in childbearing; in pain you shall bring forth children, yet your desire shall be for your husband, and he shall rule over you." 17 And to the man he said, "Because you have listened to the voice of your wife, and have eaten of the tree about which I commanded you, 'You shall not eat of it,' cursed is the ground because of you; in toil you shall eat of it all the days of your life; 18 thorns and thistles it shall bring forth for you; and you shall eat the plants of the field. 19 By the sweat of your face you shall eat bread until you return to the ground, for out of it you were taken; you are dust, and to dust you shall return." 20 The man named his wife Eve, because she was the mother of all living. 21 And the LORD God made garments of skins for the man and for his wife, and clothed them. 22 Then the LORD God said, "See, the man has become like one of us, knowing good and evil; and now, he might reach out his hand and take also from the tree of life, and eat, and live forever"—23 therefore the LORD God sent him forth from the garden of Eden, to till the ground from which he was taken. 24 He drove out the man; and at the east of the garden of Eden he placed the cherubim, and a sword flaming and turning to guard the way to the tree of life.

A STORY WITH A talking animal is by definition a fable. This story is from the period of the Babylonian exile in 587 BCE.[1] It is not referred to in any biblical passages prior to this time. Thus we find it referenced in the work of the prophet Ezekiel who is writing at the time of the Babylonian exile. Ezekiel 28:13—"You were in Eden, the garden of God; every precious stone was your covering, carnelian, chrysolite, and moonstone, beryl, onyx, and jasper, sapphire, turquoise, and emerald; and worked in gold were your settings and your engravings. On the day that you were created they

---

1. Blenkinsopp, *The Pentateuch*, 63–67.

were prepared." Ezekiel 31:9—"I made it beautiful with its mass of branches, the envy of all the trees of Eden that were in the garden of God."[2]

"Eating" is a euphemism for sexual activity.[3] The couple's partaking of the fruit thus leaves them naked. The trees and snake are goddess symbols of fertility. The snake as well as God in this fable represents the power of rivalry that the Hebrew people entered into and are subject to themselves as they copy their neighbors' cultures and religions. The story captures the expulsion of a couple from the Garden of Eden which is indeed the story of Israel who was exiled in 721 BCE by Assyria, and again in 587 BCE by Babylon.

Here we have a display of mimetic rivalry disclosed to us as the snake's argument for why God does not want them to eat of the tree at the middle of the garden for if they do *"you will be like God"* (v. 5). Here is the "double bind of imitation" that René Girard has captured. We want others to copy us for our own edification, yet at the same time once others do this we see them in competition with ourselves and this sets off rivalry.[4] In fact this entire fable is shot through and through with rivalry. Note that the snake's first question is misdirection (v. 1). In the following verse the woman misquotes God (see Genesis 3:16–17). And it culminates with a God who expels them from the garden, which entirely contradicts the God of Genesis 1, who makes humankind in God's image (see Genesis 1:26). This talking snake fable represents the reality of the double bind we are in as imitators of one another.

The point of this fable is that we cannot win at this game of imitation. The claim of eyes being opened and seeing in this fable is a lie. It is the blinding power of rivalry in this fable that keeps everyone at odds and utterly alienated from one another. It is a fable that captures what Richard Dawkins has claimed about evolution

---

2. Ibid.

3. Ibid., 65.

4. Girard, *Things Hidden Since the Foundation of the World*, 290–1. Also see Girard, *Violence and the Sacred*, 146–7.

## Genesis 3

in his work *The Blind Watchmaker*—namely that evolution has no design and is blind.[5] We are the products of evolution.

This fable also opens up for us an observation that Eric Fromm once made regarding idols. Recall that the gods and goddesses are all human-made idols that the Israelites try to copy. Fromm argues that it does not matter the number of idols, what matters is that in grasping at the thing, the idol, we give it power over us. This results in our alienation from one another and cuts off our ability to live for others, which is the essential point of our life and being.[6]

There is no death in this fable. But we are left with division. There is no reconciliation between the man and woman and God. The fable leaves us with unresolved blind human rivalry—rivalry that sets up violence and death and the entire process of scapegoating—taking out our frustrations on a victim. And this is what Israel finally came to know after so many years, ending in yet another major exile with the Babylonian captivity.

---

5. Dawkins, *The Blind Watchmaker*, 9.
6. Fromm, *The Sane Society*, 112.

# Leviticus 16

20 When he has finished atoning for the holy place and the tent of meeting and the altar, he shall present the live goat. 21 Then Aaron shall lay both his hands on the head of the live goat, and confess over it all the iniquities of the people of Israel, and all their transgressions, all their sins, putting them on the head of the goat, and sending it away into the wilderness by means of someone designated for the task. 22 The goat shall bear on itself all their iniquities to a barren region; and the goat shall be set free in the wilderness.

THIS IS A RITUAL of ancient Israel that attempted to atone for the sins of the people by their priests. The ritual entails the priest laying his hands on the head of a goat and confessing all the sins of the people. Then the goat was set free in the wilderness to fend for its own life, most likely to die at the hands of a predator. From this ritual we get the term "scapegoat," the one who becomes the victim of human aggressions.

The scapegoat ritual illustrates what René Girard recognized as the central function of religion, namely as a preventative against human violence.[1] However, the paradox that Girard identified in religion is this: the more people believe they have achieved mastery over their own violence, the more their violence increases.[2] By creating a ritual to deal with human violence we are left with an image of our own human violence to copy and an image of a God who demands the sacrifice of life.

---

1. Girard, *Violence and the Sacred*, 23.
2. Ibid., 135.

## LEVITICUS 16

The problem with our human rivalry is that it produces scapegoats whom we do not foresee as victims.[3] There is blindness in our scapegoating, not unlike the blindness Dawkins observes in evolution. Girard observes that the sign of impending revolutions and violence is the level at which we resist knowledge of our own human scapegoat mechanism.[4] What I find with Girard's insight on the scapegoat mechanism is that the violence we find in the Old Testament can now be seen from a new level of naiveté instead of the one of literalists. Whereas the literalists have copied this violence and have subscribed it to their god, the editors more likely kept these violent scenes within their writing as a reminder of human violence. Rather than hiding and denying our scapegoating, the editors of the bible confront us with our violence and cause us to reflect on our own world order today and note our patterns of scapegoating instead of denying them.

---

3 Girard, *Things Hidden Since the Foundation of the World*, 129.
4 Girard, *The Scapegoat*, 114.

# Numbers 25

1 While Israel was staying at Shittim, the people began to have sexual relations with the women of Moab. 2 These invited the people to the sacrifices of their gods, and the people ate and bowed down to their gods. 3 Thus Israel yoked itself to the Baal of Peor, and the LORD's anger was kindled against Israel. 4 The LORD said to Moses, "Take all the chiefs of the people, and impale them in the sun before the LORD, in order that the fierce anger of the LORD may turn away from Israel." 5 And Moses said to the judges of Israel, "Each of you shall kill any of your people who have yoked themselves to the Baal of Peor." 6 Just then one of the Israelites came and brought a Midianite woman into his family, in the sight of Moses and in the sight of the whole congregation of the Israelites, while they were weeping at the entrance of the tent of meeting. 7 When Phinehas son of Eleazar, son of Aaron the priest, saw it, he got up and left the congregation. Taking a spear in his hand, 8 he went after the Israelite man into the tent, and pierced the two of them, the Israelite and the woman, through the belly. So the plague was stopped among the people of Israel. 9 Nevertheless those that died by the plague were twenty-four thousand. 10 The LORD spoke to Moses, saying: 11 "Phinehas son of Eleazar, son of Aaron the priest, has turned back my wrath from the Israelites by manifesting such zeal among them on my behalf that in my jealousy I did not consume the Israelites.

THE ABOVE PASSAGE IS one of the most violent scenes you will find in the bible and yet it is perhaps the least talked about. This passage needs to be revisited in light of Girard's work on scapegoating and human violence rooted in mimetic rivalry. The socio-historical context of this passage is the period after the Babylonian exile. In this period, we will find two diverging reactions to the Israelites' experience of exile, one of bitter violent separatists, and one that reveals a God of peace and order who seeks human reconciliation.

The reading of the above passage as a literal *prescription* made by God—through a literalist interpretation—has given rise to an anti-Semitic, anti-race, anti-homosexual, anti-abortion, and anti-taxation movement in America known as the Phineas Priesthood, named after the priest in verse 7, who murders the couple.[1] This is an example of what James Alison calls "violent idolatry" and "idolatrous literalism."[2]

Read from a Girardian viewpoint we discover that Numbers 25 is indeed a *description* of human violence that illustrates the blindness inherent in the scapegoat mechanism. By avoiding these texts we fail to discover what Philip Jenkins so aptly observed in approaching these dark texts in the bible—"What people hear depends on who is doing the hearing. We see (and hear) things not as *they* are, but as *we* are."[3] By engaging the violence in the bible from the perspective of evolution and the mimetic rivalry in the human condition, we can discover what James Alison describes as "the joy of being wrong." By realizing we ourselves are the products of mimetic rivalry and scapegoating, we can discover that the scriptures are indeed designed to release us from our identities rooted in the violence and the making of victims.[4]

With evolution and the problem of human mimetic rivalry as our lens we can now move to what Paul Ricœur calls a second level of naiveté. At this second level of naiveté the symbols in a story no longer confront us head on and blind us. At the second level of naiveté we realize that we can only believe by interpreting and breaking through the myth set before us.[5] Here the story of Numbers 25 is clearly an illustration of human violence and scapegoating

1. En.wikipedia.org/wiki/Phineas_Priesthood
2. Alison, *Faith Beyond Resentment*, 103.
3. Jenkins, *Laying Down the Sword*, 235.
4. Alison, *The Joy of Being Wrong*, 22–63.
5. Ricœur, *The Symbolism of Evil*, 352.

and a projection of this human violence unto a god who is none other than the idols we have observed being made throughout the Hebrew Bible by the Israelites. Here we can strengthen our eyes and minds to see these dynamics at work in human propaganda and acts of violence today.

# Genesis 1–2

1 In the beginning when God created the heavens and the earth, 2 the earth was a formless void and darkness covered the face of the deep, while a wind from God swept over the face of the waters. 3 Then God said, "Let there be light"; and there was light. 4 And God saw that the light was good; and God separated the light from the darkness. 5 God called the light Day, and the darkness he called Night. And there was evening and there was morning, the first day. 6 And God said, "Let there be a dome in the midst of the waters, and let it separate the waters from the waters." 7 So God made the dome and separated the waters that were under the dome from the waters that were above the dome. And it was so. 8 God called the dome Sky. And there was evening and there was morning, the second day. 9 And God said, "Let the waters under the sky be gathered together into one place, and let the dry land appear." And it was so. 10 God called the dry land Earth, and the waters that were gathered together he called Seas. And God saw that it was good. 11 Then God said, "Let the earth put forth vegetation: plants yielding seed, and fruit trees of every kind on earth that bear fruit with the seed in it." And it was so. 12 The earth brought forth vegetation: plants yielding seed of every kind, and trees of every kind bearing fruit with the seed in it. And God saw that it was good. 13 And there was evening and there was morning, the third day. 14 And God said, "Let there be lights in the dome of the sky to separate the day from the night; and let them be for signs and for seasons and for days and years, 15 and let them be lights in the dome of the sky to give light upon the earth." And it was so. 16 God made the two great lights—the greater light to rule the day and the lesser light to rule the night—and the stars. 17 God set them in the dome

of the sky to give light upon the earth, 18 to rule over the day and over the night, and to separate the light from the darkness. And God saw that it was good. 19 And there was evening and there was morning, the fourth day. 20 And God said, "Let the waters bring forth swarms of living creatures, and let birds fly above the earth across the dome of the sky." 21 So God created the great sea monsters and every living creature that moves, of every kind, with which the waters swarm, and every winged bird of every kind. And God saw that it was good. 22 God blessed them, saying, "Be fruitful and multiply and fill the waters in the seas, and let birds multiply on the earth." 23 And there was evening and there was morning, the fifth day. 24 And God said, "Let the earth bring forth living creatures of every kind: cattle and creeping things and wild animals of the earth of every kind." And it was so. 25 God made the wild animals of the earth of every kind, and the cattle of every kind, and everything that creeps upon the ground of every kind. And God saw that it was good. 26 Then God said, "Let us make humankind in our image, according to our likeness; and let them have dominion over the fish of the sea, and over the birds of the air, and over the cattle, and over all the wild animals of the earth, and over every creeping thing that creeps upon the earth." 27 So God created humankind in his image, in the image of God he created them; male and female he created them. 28 God blessed them, and God said to them, "Be fruitful and multiply, and fill the earth and subdue it; and have dominion over the fish of the sea and over the birds of the air and over every living thing that moves upon the earth." 29 God said, "See, I have given you every plant yielding seed that is upon the face of all the earth, and every tree with seed in its fruit; you shall have them for food. 30 And to every beast of the earth, and to every bird of the air, and to everything that creeps on the earth, everything that has the breath of life, I have given every green plant for food." And it was so. 31 God saw everything that he had made, and indeed, it was very good. And there was evening and there was morning, the sixth day.

# Genesis 1–2

2:1 Thus the heavens and the earth were finished, and all their multitude. 2 And on the seventh day God finished the work that he had done, and he rested on the seventh day from all the work that he had done. 3 So God blessed the seventh day and hallowed it, because on it God rested from all the work that he had done in creation.

THE SOCIO-HISTORICAL CONTEXT OF this story, as with the story of Genesis 3, the Garden of Eden story, is the period following the Babylonian exile that ended in approximately 500 BCE.[1] "The deep" which God creates out of is *"ti-home"* in Hebrew, borrowed from the name of the Babylonian goddess Tiamat. Genesis 1 represents a radical revision of the Babylonian account of creation given in *The Enuma Elish Story*. In *The Enuma Elish* we find the rivalry between the god Marduk and the goddess Tiamat. *The Enuma Elish* represents the mimetic violence of humans portrayed in a battle myth where Marduk is the divine warrior who subdues and kills Tiamat, using her slain body to create the world.[2]

The main subject of Genesis 1 is not creation but God. Only now, in Genesis 1, God is not a violent creator like Marduk, the divine warrior. Genesis 1 replaces the violent warrior god with the God who makes creation "good." It took the Israelites approximately 3,500 years of their 4,000-year biblical history to arrive at the writing of this story. It demonstrates what René Girard has observed once the bible is read from the viewpoint of humanity emerging from a mimetic rivalry, that "the Bible (is) permeated by a single dynamic movement away from sacrifice."[3] Within human evolution Genesis 1 is a remarkable break from the myth of order created through violence.

In verse 26 we find the making of humankind in God's image. Here is a complete reversal of the rivalry that we find in Genesis 3:5, where the serpent portrays God as someone who would be envious if humans were to become "like" God. In Genesis 1:26

---

1. Blenkinsopp, *The Pentateuch*, 64–65.
2. Matthews and Benjamin, *Old Testament Parallels*, 6–15.
3. Girard, *Things Hidden Since the Foundation of the World*, 239.

there is no rivalry between God and humans over likeness. This is highly significant in terms of mimesis; for *it removes the rivalry* we have noted and observed thus far in human nature, which results when humans copy one another. Thus, the story concludes with God who is not in rivalry, which follows from a God who creates without entering into the violent destruction of others.

What we have in Genesis 1 is not a literal account of how creation has come about, but rather, how a non-violent image of God has now been revealed through the Israelite's experience of exile in Babylon. With it the Israelites were able to establish their own sense of order, time, and space, and a seven-day week, which was the foundation for linear time-keeping for our culture. No longer are humans simply traveling in a mythic eternal return with their violent gods. As the Israelites emerge from exile they discover a God whose life is found by creating order without violence.

On the seventh day God rested and declared that day "hallowed"—holy. Genesis 1 provides the foundation for the Sabbath—a day of rest and revitalization, time and space for worshipping a God who does not rival us for being made in God's very likeness. Today multinational corporate economic forces drive worker competition and the accumulation of wealth. We once again find this sense of Sabbath ignored. Today we hear talk of the seven-day work week. The corporate greed of our day returns us to Babylon, away from the order of life revealed by God in Genesis 1.

In Genesis 1 God creates through a *Word* by speaking "let there be." "Word" is *dabar* in Hebrew, which also translates as "event." Yet this *Word* has much more work to do. For the *Word* of this God may make us in God's likeness, but this *Word* has not yet been revealed to us in human form in one whom we could copy and be like. In order for this further act of creation to occur the salvation story needs to continue in the person of Jesus Christ.

# Daniel 1

1 In the third year of the reign of King Jehoiakim of Judah, King Nebuchadnezzar of Babylon came to Jerusalem and besieged it. 2 The Lord let King Jehoiakim of Judah fall into his power, as well as some of the vessels of the house of God. These he brought to the land of Shinar, and placed the vessels in the treasury of his gods. 3 Then the king commanded his palace master Ashpenaz to bring some of the Israelites of the royal family and of the nobility, 4 young men without physical defect and handsome, versed in every branch of wisdom, endowed with knowledge and insight, and competent to serve in the king's palace; they were to be taught the literature and language of the Chaldeans. 5 The king assigned them a daily portion of the royal rations of food and wine. They were to be educated for three years, so that at the end of that time they could be stationed in the king's court. 6 Among them were Daniel, Hananiah, Mishael, and Azariah, from the tribe of Judah. 7 The palace master gave them other names: Daniel he called Belteshazzar, Hananiah he called Shadrach, Mishael he called Meshach, and Azariah he called Abednego. 8 But Daniel resolved that he would not defile himself with the royal rations of food and wine; so he asked the palace master to allow him not to defile himself. 9 Now God allowed Daniel to receive favor and compassion from the palace master. 10 The palace master said to Daniel, "I am afraid of my lord the king; he has appointed your food and your drink. If he should see you in poorer condition than the other young men of your own age, you would endanger my head with the king." 11 Then Daniel asked the guard whom the palace master had appointed over Daniel, Hananiah, Mishael, and Azariah: 12 "Please test your servants for ten days. Let us be given vegetables to eat and water to

drink. 13 You can then compare our appearance with the appearance of the young men who eat the royal rations, and deal with your servants according to what you observe." 14 So he agreed to this proposal and tested them for ten days. 15 At the end of ten days it was observed that they appeared better and fatter than all the young men who had been eating the royal rations. 16 So the guard continued to withdraw their royal rations and the wine they were to drink, and gave them vegetables. 17 To these four young men God gave knowledge and skill in every aspect of literature and wisdom; Daniel also had insight into all visions and dreams. 18 At the end of the time that the king had set for them to be brought in, the palace master brought them into the presence of Nebuchadnezzar, 19 and the king spoke with them. And among them all, no one was found to compare with Daniel, Hananiah, Mishael, and Azariah; therefore they were stationed in the king's court. 20 In every matter of wisdom and understanding concerning which the king inquired of them, he found them ten times better than all the magicians and enchanters in his whole kingdom. 21 And Daniel continued there until the first year of King Cyrus.

DURING THE RULE OF Antioches IV Epiphanies, 167 to 164 BCE, the Seleucids desecrated the temple in Jerusalem with a pagan altar that violated the Israelites' laws on food and purity.[1] The book imports the legendary figure Daniel, whose name means "God is my judge," from the time of the Babylonian exile, to provide a story of resistance against the oppression of the Seleucids. Chapter 1 of Daniel immediately addresses the issue of the Israelite's observance of dietary law as Daniel and his three friends refuse to eat the diet of King Nebuchadnezzar. Those arguing to be vegetarian need not look further than the book of Daniel. After a ten-day vegetable diet Daniel and his friends, now known as Shadrach, Meshach, and Abednego, all appear "ten times better than all the magicians and enchanters in [the] whole kingdom" (v. 20).

1. Smith-Christopher, "The Book of Daniel," 26.

## Daniel 1

As with Joseph in Genesis 41:25, Daniel possesses the ability to understand visions and dreams (v. 17). Walter Brueggemann makes the observation that the powers of oppression do not sleep in peace, but rather always live in "nightmare turned to policy" as they worry about reprisal from those whom they are trying to control.[2] Thus like Pharaoh with Joseph, King Nebuchadnezzar employs the dream interpreting powers of Daniel.

Daniel's ability to fast and his gift of dream interpretation lead him to a powerful form of non-violent resistance against King Nebuchadnezzar's rule. Daniel outlasts the rule of both King Nebuchadnezzar and King Darius (Chapter 6), until the Persian King Cyrus would conquer Babylon and set the Israelite captives free. Again this is all an imported story, but the narrative of Daniel never stops short of complete non-violent resistance to oppression until it is entirely defeated. In terms of mimetic theory Daniel represents the ability to resist copying and complying with the powers of oppression that try to change people's identity right down to their very names.

Daniel was a source that Mohandas Gandhi drew from in his non-violent resistance that he called *ahimsa*.[3] For Gandhi fasting was more than political, it was a duty done out of agony for the oppressed.[4] Yet his fast turned back the power of British imperialism over India.

---

2. Brueggemann, *Journey to the Common Good*, 7.
3. Smith-Christopher, "The Book of Daniel," 94–95.
4. Merton, *Gandhi on Non-Violence*, 76.

# Daniel 9

1 In the first year of Darius son of Ahasuerus, by birth a Mede, who became king over the realm of the Chaldeans—2 in the first year of his reign, I, Daniel, perceived in the books the number of years that, according to the word of the LORD to the prophet Jeremiah, must be fulfilled for the devastation of Jerusalem, namely, seventy years. 3 Then I turned to the Lord God, to seek an answer by prayer and supplication with fasting and sackcloth and ashes. 4 I prayed to the LORD my God and made confession, saying, "Ah, Lord, great and awesome God, keeping covenant and steadfast love with those who love you and keep your commandments, 5 we have sinned and done wrong, acted wickedly and rebelled, turning aside from your commandments and ordinances. 6 We have not listened to your servants the prophets, who spoke in your name to our kings, our princes, and our ancestors, and to all the people of the land.

7 "Righteousness is on your side, O Lord, but open shame, as at this day, falls on us, the people of Judah, the inhabitants of Jerusalem, and all Israel, those who are near and those who are far away, in all the lands to which you have driven them, because of the treachery that they have committed against you. 8 Open shame, O LORD, falls on us, our kings, our officials, and our ancestors, because we have sinned against you. 9 To the Lord our God belong mercy and forgiveness, for we have rebelled against him, 10 and have not obeyed the voice of the LORD our God by following his laws, which he set before us by his servants the prophets.

11 "All Israel has transgressed your law and turned aside, refusing to obey your voice. So the curse and the oath written in the law of Moses, the servant of God, have been poured out upon us, because we have sinned

## Daniel 9

against you. 12 He has confirmed his words, which he spoke against us and against our rulers, by bringing upon us a calamity so great that what has been done against Jerusalem has never before been done under the whole heaven. 13 Just as it is written in the law of Moses, all this calamity has come upon us. We did not entreat the favor of the LORD our God, turning from our iniquities and reflecting on his fidelity. 14 So the LORD kept watch over this calamity until he brought it upon us. Indeed, the LORD our God is right in all that he has done; for we have disobeyed his voice.

15 "And now, O Lord our God, who brought your people out of the land of Egypt with a mighty hand and made your name renowned even to this day—we have sinned, we have done wickedly. 16 O Lord, in view of all your righteous acts, let your anger and wrath, we pray, turn away from your city Jerusalem, your holy mountain; because of our sins and the iniquities of our ancestors, Jerusalem and your people have become a disgrace among all our neighbors. 17 Now therefore, O our God, listen to the prayer of your servant and to his supplication, and for your own sake, Lord, let your face shine upon your desolated sanctuary. 18 Incline your ear, O my God, and hear. Open your eyes and look at our desolation and the city that bears your name. We do not present our supplication before you on the ground of our righteousness, but on the ground of your great mercies. 19 O Lord, hear; O Lord, forgive; O Lord, listen and act and do not delay! For your own sake, O my God, because your city and your people bear your name!"

VERSE 2 SHOWS US that the book of Daniel is drawing from the prophet Jeremiah as it provides us with Jeremiah's estimation of how long the Israelites were in exile in Babylon—seventy years. We read in Jeremiah 29:10, "For thus says the LORD: Only when Babylon's seventy years are completed will I visit you, and I will fulfill to you my promise and bring you back to this place." This section of chapter 9 uses the Babylonian exile as the setting for Daniel's confession/prayer to God. Keep in mind that this literary context from approximately 587 BCE to 512 BCE is being imported to address the socio-historical context of the Israelites' oppression by the Seleucid Dynasty in 167 to 164 BCE. As we shall see in the next passage, Daniel 9:24 will provide a reference of seventy weeks for the occupation of the temple in Jerusalem by the Seleucids.

Why does a book that portrays characters with such a strong non-violent resistance to an occupation by foreign powers end up with a confession about Israel's past history? It is one thing to see the obvious idolatry of power from those outside our group. It is quite another thing to recognize the idols of power that destroy not only our own group, but also our very selves. Daniel's prayer as confession reveals the power of prayer to shed light on the blindness inherent in our human condition of mimesis. In the above passage we see how Israel has been unable to follow the commandments and laws of God in verses 5, 10, and 11. Everything that the prophet Samuel said would happen to the Israelites as a nation at the start of this book has come true. In verse 6 it is confessed that the people would not listen to *any* of their own prophets, rulers, and ancestors.

The prayer/confession discloses to us an ambiguous image of a God who is love (v. 4) yet also a God of anger and wrath (v. 16). Verse 15 recalls the Exodus story of Israelite deliverance from Egypt. Verses 16–18 take us into Jerusalem, the context of the temple and its desecration by the Seleucids. Verse 19 ends with the hope that only God will deliver them for the sake of a city and people who bear God's name.

Our religious, national, and political ideologies can easily see the enemy and oppressor outside our in-group, but we are mostly blind to powers that divide us against our own neighbor and the common good of our own culture. The United States is an illustration of this. We have been "defending democracy" for fifty years all over the globe as multination corporate power has drawn upon our military industrial complex, the CIA, and NSA to secure its financial interests. Now this power has come full circle and its immense wealth and monopolies dismantle democracy through the media it controls and the elections it buys. Instead of being exiled,

## Daniel 9

we are indeed more like the actual socio-historical context of Daniel as the powers that be now descend upon us.

The power in this passage lies in how *prayer as confession* can be an exercise in breaking through the denial of what is taking place all around us. Prayer is not merely petitioning God for what we want as if God is a perpetual form of Santa Claus. Prayer is also confession that has the ability to take the blinders off the mimetic rivalry we live in—especially in our sports-saturated culture that functions like a religion celebrating the divide and conquer politics that is being played out upon us.

> It draws us into a timeless world in which only the play of the game matters: the alternation of innings, the repeated circling toward home; we can relax in the stands and let the tension build slowly, secure in the knowledge it will be back tomorrow or next week or next year. Mortality there is, to be sure, and even danger, but the kind we understand—the kind that's already incorporated into the baseball history and folklore. It has a calming effect. There is, of course, the more disturbing world of crime, of drugs and booze and contracts and owners and endorsements and gambling and . . .but, here, inside, all is well.
> 
> Alas, games do end, finally. Darkness comes, the batter grounds to second for the third out in the bottom of the ninth, the sudden home run wins in the twelfth. Then we exit, reluctantly, from the park, out of the magic circle into real time where life awaits—and there's nothing easy about that.[1]

On any given weekend in America during football season there will be more people gathered into stadiums than in all places of worship combined. For many people it is hard to tell where the line between Fox News and Fox Sports begins and ends. One world bleeds into the next. We carry our team rivalry into our political rivalry. We forget that one is a game and the other is life. Steve Almond has managed to make this confession of the game:

---

1. Goldstein, "Take Me Back to the Ball Game," 155.

## Salvation Story

When we root for a team, the conscious desire is to see them win, to bask in reflected glory. But the unconscious function of fandom is, I think, just the opposite. It's a form of surrender to our essential helplessness in the universal order. In an age of scientific assurance, people still yearn for spiritual struggle. Fandom allows us to fire our faith in the forge of loss. Because our teams inevitably do lose. And this experience forms the bedrock of our identification.

Backing a team helps Americans, in particular, contend with the unease of living in the most competitive society on earth, a society in which we're socialized to feel like losers. That's the special sauce capitalism puts on the burgers. It's how you turn your citizens into workers and consumers. You convince them that they are forever falling behind. Losing time. Losing money. Losing status. Losing hair. Losing potency. Losing the edge. We feel we're losing all the time, simply by failing to win. We squander our talents, we mismanage the clock, we choke in the clutch. Our teams enact the public dramas that we experience as struggles to transcend our own private defects.

We need look no further for evidence than to the proliferation of sports talk radio. Anyone who's listened to this format will tell you nothing lights up the phone lines like a crushing loss. And what one hears in the callers' voices, beneath the bluster, is actually quite moving: an effort to preserve belief amid the tribulation of defeat.[2]

Tucked into the religion of football is the belief in violent rivalry. In Daniel we find that ultimately the violent is not transcended. God is still viewed as a God of wrath. The hope remains that the wrath of such a God—who is the projection of our game—will be visited upon our rivals. This game does not change in the salvation story until we reach the person of Jesus Christ.

> Daniel 9:21 while I was speaking in prayer, the man Gabriel, whom I had seen before in a vision, came to me in swift flight at the time of the evening sacrifice. 22 He

---

2. Almond, *Against Football*, 60–61.

came and said to me, "Daniel, I have now come out to give you wisdom and understanding. 23 At the beginning of your supplications a word went out, and I have come to declare it, for you are greatly beloved. So consider the word and understand the vision:

24 "Seventy weeks are decreed for your people and your holy city: to finish the transgression, to put an end to sin, and to atone for iniquity, to bring in everlasting righteousness, to seal both vision and prophet, and to anoint a most holy place. 25 Know therefore and understand: from the time that the word went out to restore and rebuild Jerusalem until the time of an anointed prince, there shall be seven weeks; and for sixty-two weeks it shall be built again with streets and moat, but in a troubled time. 26 After the sixty-two weeks, an anointed one shall be cut off and shall have nothing, and the troops of the prince who is to come shall destroy the city and the sanctuary. Its end shall come with a flood, and to the end there shall be war. Desolations are decreed. 27 He shall make a strong covenant with many for one week, and for half of the week he shall make sacrifice and offering cease; and in their place shall be an abomination that desolates, until the decreed end is poured out upon the desolator."

Daniel receives an answer to his prayer/confession from a man named Gabriel whom he had previously seen in a vision (v. 21). Daniel receives a time-line regarding the duration in which the oppression will last for seventy weeks. Note that in the previous passage of 9:1–19 we read the literary reference to the prophet Jeremiah in verse 2 and its revealing of the length of the Babylonian exile being seventy years. Here the number of seventy weeks (v. 24) is referring to the actual socio-historical context of the Seleucid Dynasty's occupation of the Israelites in Jerusalem and the restoration of their temple. The seventy weeks is then followed by a division of time; seven weeks of occupation and sixty-two weeks of restoration (v. 25). A covenant, agreement between God and Israel, is to be made the seventieth week (v. 27).

## SALVATION STORY

I am treating this passage because once upon a time the preacher John Nelson Darby (1800–1882), created an entire new religious movement out of his speculation over this passage. Darby divided the seventy weeks into seven distinct "dispensations" of time allotted by God, devising an entire lens for reading the bible in anticipation of "the end time." This bible was published by Cyrus I. Scofield in 1909 and became known as *The Scofield Bible*.[3] According to Darby we are living in the final week, the last dispensation of time. In this time Darby devised a scheme where believers would be "raptured" into heaven while those left behind will suffer great tribulation, death, and destruction until Christ finally returns with his chosen for his final reign upon earth (for a thousand years—thus the name "millennialism") after which comes the final judgment.[4] Darby's religious movement found its counterpart in the political movement of Zionism founded by Theodore Herzl (1860–1904), who believed that Jews must live apart from Gentiles in Israel in order to avoid persecution. Darby has Christ returning to the temple in Israel, thus the state must be restored (as well as the temple).

Followers of Darby's church, The Plymouth Brethren, have evolved into Christian Zionism, a religion seeking the end time, while making the modern state of Israel the focus of Christ's return. Christian Zionism is tied into the entire Palestinian/Israeli conflict, as the Christian Zionists maintain that all of Palestine belongs to the current state of Israel.[5] More troubling is the historical reality of how these forces have played into the holocaust.[6]

3. Rossing, *The Rapture Exposed*, 22–25.
4. Ibid.
5. Ruether and Ruether, *The Wrath of Jonah*, 80–84.
6. Ibid., 60–61. Also see Black, *The Transfer Agreement*. Black documents the ideological struggle between two groups within Zionism—the Mapai, who work for the transfer of 60,000 German Jews to Palestine in 1933 in exchange for an allotted amount of money in German bank accounts, held by families, and the Revisionist movement that held a world boycott against Hitler's Third Reich. The effect of the boycott was strong and literally brought the nation into a potential civil war and overthrow of the Reich. Ultimately, the Mapai succeeded in forcing through their plan, freeing 60,000 Jews to leave for Palestine, while leaving behind six million Jews to die. The transfer agreement has been one of the biggest points of debate and division within the Jewish community.

## Daniel 9

Most recently the U.S. wars in Iraq and Afghanistan were the context for popularizing this religion in the *Left Behind* series of books written by Tim Lahaye and Jerry Jenkins. It is important to see how the use of Daniel 9 as a lens for reading the bible has managed to return it to violent mythology. *Millennialism, dispensationalism, the rapture, the apocalypse,* these are all code words for religious violence where the bible has been interpreted as a continuation of the ancient battle myth.

In verse 26 we find *flood* and *war* being visited upon the Israelites' oppressors. In the rapture religion these forces are tied to predetermined outcomes as in ancient mythologies that create sacrificial victims. Meanwhile it functions today as the cover for economic and political gain through war now instigated through terrorism. The importance of Daniel 9 in light of mimetic rivalry is that it illustrates for us once again its dynamic that blinds people to the power of their own violence. In our time the sea level rises from human induced climate change (flood), yet propaganda from the fossil fuel industry in the media spreads denial of this. Once again terrorists are being armed by the powers that be and increases are proposed for the military budget. It is much easier to identify and resist the idols that are outside of us—as King Nebuchadnezzar's statue of gold was for Daniel and his friends. It is quite another thing to be able to see the idols of power in our own culture that lead us back into re-creating the violent battle myths of old. From a biblical perspective, we cannot break out of our blindness to violence unless we see from the life, death, and resurrection of Jesus Christ.

# John 1

1 In the beginning was the Word, and the Word was with God, and the Word was God. 2 He was in the beginning with God. 3 All things came into being through him, and without him not one thing came into being. What has come into being 4 in him was life, and the life was the light of all people. 5 The light shines in the darkness, and the darkness did not overcome it.

6 There was a man sent from God, whose name was John. 7 He came as a witness to testify to the light, so that all might believe through him. 8 He himself was not the light, but he came to testify to the light. 9 The true light, which enlightens everyone, was coming into the world.

10 He was in the world, and the world came into being through him; yet the world did not know him. 11 He came to what was his own, and his own people did not accept him. 12 But to all who received him, who believed in his name, he gave power to become children of God, 13 who were born, not of blood or of the will of the flesh or of the will of man, but of God.

14 And the Word became flesh and lived among us, and we have seen his glory, the glory as of a father's only son, full of grace and truth. 15 (John testified to him and cried out, "This was he of whom I said, 'He who comes after me ranks ahead of me because he was before me.'") 16 From his fullness we have all received, grace upon grace. 17 The law indeed was given through Moses; grace and truth came through Jesus Christ. 18 No one has ever seen God. It is God the only Son, who is close to the Father's heart, who has made him known.

JOHN'S ACCOUNT OF THE gospel is written approximately in the time frame of 90 to 100 AD. It is the latest of the four gospel

# JOHN 1

accounts yet the only account which brings together the illustration of a non-violent creator God from Genesis 1 with the birth of Jesus. John is a deeply Jewish work—a work written to Jews who were expelled from the synagogue by fellow Jews for their faith in Jesus Christ. John 9:22 and 12:42 reference being put out of the synagogue for believing that Jesus is the Messiah—the one who comes to fulfill the reign of God on earth. Thus we find in verse 11 the mention of Jesus Christ not being accepted by his own people. Yet the Jewish community of John does accept Jesus Christ. This careful reading of the work is important lest we repeat the anti-Semitism that the church once held.

"Word" in Greek is *logos*, yet John imports the Hebrew sense of "word," *dabar*, that we found in the Hebrew writing of Genesis 1. In verse 1 we find Jesus as "the Word" who exists with God at the start of creation. Yet, this created order that humans are a part of (v. 13), is not the source of life. Instead we find the claim that "life" is in this Word become flesh (v. 4). This Word become flesh is like a light in what otherwise is implied to be a world of "darkness," darkness which could not overcome this light (v. 5). Jesus Christ is the non-violent God of Genesis 1 who is not part of the mimetic order of human rivalry and who has come into "the world" (vs. 9-10). Thus Jesus Christ is light amid the darkness of human rivalry, violence, and death.

John the Baptist is referenced in verses 5 and 15. These verses point to the preaching of John the Baptist to the Jews about the coming of the Messiah—their savior, and his baptizing of people. In verse 12 we find that those who receive Jesus Christ are given a new identity as "children of God." This Word comes not only to be born in the person of Jesus but comes to be the source of our receiving "life" that is not based on the dis-order of our mimetic rivalry.

Verses 17 and 18 speak of the law through Moses and grace through Jesus Christ. As we have seen in the Hebrew writings earlier, the law only points to the failure of the Israelites in keeping it. Grace, which is mercy and forgiveness, is now given in Jesus Christ as the means to live beyond the death due to our mimetic rivalry.

It is our alienated self in the dis-ordered world of our rivalry, conflict, violence, and death that is now being offered a new common identity in Jesus Christ. This is the "grace upon grace" (v. 16), not only are we forgiven for being who we are as violent creatures in the first order of creation, but now in the creation of the Word made flesh we are offered a new life-giving identity in Jesus Christ as children of God.

Once we read Genesis 1 as the revealing of a God who does not create out of violence, we can begin to see the dynamic of "the Word made flesh" in Jesus Christ. Literalism has missed this reading of Genesis 1, and therefore misses the non-violent identity of the Word made flesh—Jesus Christ. This connection in what has been traditionally referred to as the *incarnation*, God entering into humanity, is essential if we are to grow beyond the violent use of the bible and the false Christianity of our time that fails to see the rest of humanity as the very place it shall reside in as a person of faith in Jesus Christ.

The claim of John's gospel is that the Word, the non-violent God, is the source of life for us creatures who in our evolutionary development are vexed with destructive mimetic violence. Rather than project our idols, our violent projections onto God, John's gospel offers us new identity in One who does not share in our evolutionary creaturely rivalry—Jesus Christ, who is our salvation.

# Mark 1

9 In those days Jesus came from Nazareth of Galilee and was baptized by John in the Jordan. 10 And just as he was coming up out of the water, he saw the heavens torn apart and the Spirit descending like a dove on him. 11 And a voice came from heaven, "You are my Son, the Beloved; with you I am well pleased."

BAPTISM IS AN ANCIENT ritual to signify death and rebirth—being submerged in the waters of chaos and death like the flood in the Genesis Noah story, the drowning of Pharaoh's army in the story of Exodus, and rising up out of the water into new life. The Jordan River is the boundary that for the Jewish people marks their entrance into the Promised Land. It signifies freedom and life as God's people and nation. For John to be baptizing people is highly political in two ways. First, it is a ritual that signifies national identity apart from the Roman Empire and the desire to be free from its power. Second, it signifies new life and freedom from the power of sin that at this time is tied to ritual works and sacrifices performed by the priests at the temple in Jerusalem. John is by-passing the religious system of the day and defying the power of the Empire.

Yet much more is taking place during the baptismal account of Jesus, which all of the other Gospel accounts of Matthew, Luke and John share, namely that the heavens are opened and the Spirit descends. The ancient worldview that divided and separated heaven and earth is now joined. In their DVD presentation titled *The Future of Christianity: A Startling New Vision of Hope for the 21st Century,* Thomas Keating and Ken Wilbur point out that what is impeding the spiritual development of humanity today is the inability of people to have an integral view of the world. I touched upon this earlier with the work of Walter Wink. The religious fundamentalist mindset keeps the mimetic rivalry alive by using the separated worlds of heaven and earth to declare who is "in" and who is "out"—who is saved and who is left behind.

The baptism of Jesus reveals the ongoing *incarnation* (the Word become flesh) of deity and humanity inseparably joined in Jesus Christ as the heavens are opened and the Spirit descends upon Jesus. The New Testament is the ongoing presence of the Word/Spirit in Jesus' accounts of ministry and death—the outpouring of his life into others. Our mimetic rivalry disconnects us from this incarnate and integral worldview of the New Testament. So, for example, today we find movies such as *Heaven is for Real* to promote once again the immortalizing of our selflike pagan gods, instead of an integral view of heaven and earth joined and our baptismal life signifying dying to our self and living in Jesus Christ whose life is poured out for all of humanity. A closer look at the biblical text of the New Testament will reveal an integral worldview that does not hold to the divided worlds of our mimetic rivalry. Let us continue the theme of the meaning of baptism with Paul's work in his letter to the Romans.

# Romans 6

3 Do you not know that all of us who have been baptized into Christ Jesus were baptized into his death? 4 Therefore we have been buried with him by baptism into death, so that, just as Christ was raised from the dead by the glory of the Father, so we too might walk in newness of life. 5 For if we have been united with him in a death like his, we will certainly be united with him in a resurrection like his. 6 We know that our old self was crucified with him so that the body of sin might be destroyed, and we might no longer be enslaved to sin. 7 For whoever has died is freed from sin. 8 But if we have died with Christ, we believe that we will also live with him. 9 We know that Christ, being raised from the dead, will never die again; death no longer has dominion over him. 10 The death he died, he died to sin, once for all; but the life he lives, he lives to God.

PAUL'S LETTER TO THE Romans represents his final letter and his most complete theological understanding of Jesus Christ. Martin Luther cited this passage in his writing of *The Small Catechism* in order to explain the meaning of baptism.[1] Baptism is referred to as being a *sacrament*. Christians took the word sacrament from the Roman Empire who used it as an oath of allegiance sworn by Roman soldiers to the empire. Christians subverted its meaning and used it as an allegiance to Jesus Christ. Luther cites verse 4 of the above text to define the meaning of baptism. Baptism brings newness of life through daily dying to self and rising anew to life and identity in Jesus Christ.[2] Paul goes on to develop his mean-

---

1. Luther, *The Small Catechism*, 23–25.
2. Ibid.

ing of baptism into Jesus Christ, culminating in Romans 12:5, "so we, who are many, are one body in Christ, and individually we are members one of another." Contrary to all the individualistic self-immortalizing views of after-life that we can find in ancient pagan culture and our culture today, baptism defines our life in Jesus Christ, not our self. Our life in Jesus Christ joins our identity to one another.

Martin Luther was steeped in the writings of St. Paul, especially Romans. As a Lutheran I find that Luther's understanding of baptism is the key to his view of the *incarnation*—God's Word made flesh in Jesus Christ together with God's Word/Spirit being made flesh in our humanity. Paul Althaus once observed, "Luther thus takes the deity of Christ and his incarnation more seriously than anyone since the New Testament writers themselves."[3] Thus the baptism of Jesus and our baptism are essentially the core of an *incarnate* God in Jesus Christ. Because of Jesus Christ our world is essentially integral—there is no separation of heaven and earth, and we are no longer alienated selves. This means that our life and being in Jesus Christ is now in one another. This is the foundation for such sayings from Jesus as "love one another," and "love your enemy." There is no "after-life" outside of our humanity that Christ has claimed.

I have addressed Jesus' baptism and the meaning of baptism so that as we look at some of the gospel stories we may see this incarnate identity of Jesus Christ addressing the alienated mimetic self of rivalry of others all the way to the cross and beyond into the resurrection and the coming of God's Spirit.

---

3. Althaus, *The Theology of Martin Luther*, 191.

# Mark 2

23 One sabbath he was going through the grainfields; and as they made their way his disciples began to pluck heads of grain. 24 The Pharisees said to him, "Look, why are they doing what is not lawful on the sabbath?" 25 And he said to them, "Have you never read what David did when he and his companions were hungry and in need of food? 26 He entered the house of God, when Abiathar was high priest, and ate the bread of the Presence, which it is not lawful for any but the priests to eat, and he gave some to his companions." 27 Then he said to them, "The sabbath was made for humankind, and not humankind for the sabbath; 28 so the Son of Man is lord even of the sabbath."

JESUS AND HIS DISCIPLES are breaking what the Pharisees (one of the Jewish religious groups of Jesus' day) see as a prohibition against work on the Sabbath—the Jewish day of rest. René Girard names prohibitions along with myth and sacrifice as "the pillars of primitive religion" that justify violence against a scapegoat.[1] In response to the charge from the Pharisees, in verses 25–26, Jesus references the story of David found in 1 Samuel, chapters 20 and 21, where David is fleeing from the violent pursuit of Saul. Jesus references a situation where one is in need of food because of being a refugee. Jesus reveals the violence inherent in the religious system of the Pharisees while at the same time he claims that the true purpose of the Sabbath is not to serve the human system of religion, but to serve the well-being of humanity.

By pointing out David's eating of the "bread of Presence," Jesus subverts the Pharisees' sense of the sacred. It is important to

---

1. Girard, *Things Hidden Since the Foundation of the World*, 154–5.

note here what Girard has claimed in his work, namely, that "the sacred" is the system that conceals and justifies human violence.[2] Jesus is claiming the actions of David, whose immediate hunger was more important than any religious purpose for the bread that only the priests were allowed to eat. Here let us note what Girard also observes about our human institutions of culture and religion, namely, that they build constructs around the victims of their past in order to lose sight of them, while focusing people on prohibitions.[3] Jesus has lifted up a story from his own people's history that defies the making of a victim, as David escapes the violence of Saul. Meanwhile, the Pharisees are part of the system of religion that will pursue Jesus up until his death.

The problem with Judaism at the time of Jesus is that it was now a system subservient to the power of the Roman Empire. It is like the Christianity of today's dominant culture in America that markets prosperity and the immortalizing of the self over service to humanity and care for the earth. Sabbath at the time of Jesus had been turned into the service of the Roman Empire through focusing on prohibition and ritual sacrifice over concern for the well-being of one's neighbor. In the above story, Jesus has reclaimed the real meaning of Sabbath over and against both the culture and religion of his day. Today this claim is alive as some church communities use their weekly worship time for going out into the community in order to do service to help people in need.

Dom Helder Camara, Catholic Archbishop of Brazil, once said, "When I gave food to the poor, they called me a saint. When I asked why the poor have no food, they called me a communist." Jesus is doing more than merely feeding himself and his disciples who are hungry on a Sabbath; Jesus is breaking the religious/cultural system that will also earn him many names, including enemy of the empire. The salvation story is not merely about some "do good" and "feel good" actions on the part of Jesus, it is the very confronting of our religious and cultural systems that oppress the poor, hoard power, and condone violence, while justifying

2. Girard, *Violence and the Sacred*, 262.
3. Ibid., 267.

everything through its myth, sacrifices, and prohibitions. As Jesus reclaims the meaning of Sabbath we are now well on our way into the uncovering of religion as a human system of oppression and violence.

# Mark 3

1 Again he entered the synagogue, and a man was there who had a withered hand. 2 They watched him to see whether he would cure him on the sabbath, so that they might accuse him. 3 And he said to the man who had the withered hand, "Come forward." 4 Then he said to them, "Is it lawful to do good or to do harm on the sabbath, to save life or to kill?" But they were silent. 5 He looked around at them with anger; he was grieved at their hardness of heart and said to the man, "Stretch out your hand." He stretched it out, and his hand was restored. 6 The Pharisees went out and immediately conspired with the Herodians against him, how to destroy him.

THE TIME SETTING IS Sabbath and the context is a synagogue—a place where Jews gather to conduct and receive teachings on God's Word from the Torah. Everyone in this story is Jewish. Again like our previous story the division and rivalry will be over the purpose of the Sabbath. This is the only place in the entire New Testament where you will find the mention of anger (v. 5) being connected to Jesus. This passage provides for us the exploration of Jesus' anger used as energy that seeks the truth and provides healing for another in contrast to the anger of the Pharisees and the Herodians (a political party aligned with King Herod) whose anger incites them to plot how to destroy Jesus.

Richard Rohr and Andreas Ebert write on how *anger* is the energy produced by one's perception of what is wrong and in need of correcting.[1] Add to this mimetic theory, the human need to copy, our development of identity in-groups and out-groups, and we can see how anger fits entirely into mimetic rivalry. Jesus' un-

---

1. Rohr and Ebert, *Discovering the Enneagram*, 35–49.

derstanding of the Sabbath as a source of service to those in need poses a threat to the identity of the Pharisees whose understanding of Sabbath is to protect the status quo of religion in service of the Empire. Verse 2 gives us the plot; they (the Pharisees and Herodians) are waiting to see what Jesus will do on the Sabbath. In verse 3, Jesus engages the man with a withered hand and commands him to come forward. In verse 4, we receive the search for truth on the part of Jesus—what Rohr and Ebert claim that a spiritually healthy person does with their anger. Jesus asks, "Is it lawful to do good or to do harm on the Sabbath, to save life or to kill?" This question is loaded with two levels of revelation aimed at the mimetic rivalry at hand between Jesus and the Pharisees. On the first level Jesus addresses the mimetic blindness that anger produces when it serves the defense of an in-group. The Herodians and Pharisees are watching and protecting the Sabbath of their religion. What they are blind to is the man's withered hand in need of healing. On the second level, Jesus also defines the true purpose of law in the Torah as doing a good deed for the neighbor by healing the man with a withered hand, in contrast to their intent of harming and killing Jesus. Jesus as the Word of God incarnate does not share in the violent use of human anger; rather he converts its energy into healing. At the same time Jesus reveals the destructive use of anger as the source of human violence.

The Herodians and Pharisees are silent. They cannot answer Jesus. Jesus goes to the heart of their mimetic rivalry. They cannot choose good for it undermines their anger's need to be correct about the purpose of the Sabbath. They cannot choose harm for it reveals the violence within their very selves. Verses 5 and 6 play out for us the creative use of human anger by Jesus and the subversion of mimetic rivalry into an occasion for healing.

In verse 5, Jesus grieves over the hardness of heart of the Pharisees and Herodians. Recall how, earlier, in Isaiah 6, hardness of the heart is connected to blindness. The Pharisees and Herodians cannot see the man's need for healing. Thus Jesus commands the hand to be stretched out in full view for all to see and conducts his healing for everyone to see.

## Salvation Story

As the living Word in the synagogue, not the mere written words on the Torah, Jesus restores a man's withered hand as well as the meaning of the Sabbath as the time for serving one's neighbor in need. The scene closes with the revelation of human rivalry as the source of violence as the Herodians and Pharisees now set out to destroy Jesus through a plot that will continue to the cross— where our violence shall be revealed once and for all for the whole world to see.

> Mark 3:19b Then he went home; 20 and the crowd came together again, so that they could not even eat. 21 When his family heard it, they went out to restrain him, for people were saying, "He has gone out of his mind." 22 And the scribes who came down from Jerusalem said, "He has Beelzebub, and by the ruler of the demons he casts out demons." 23 And he called them to him, and spoke to them in parables, "How can Satan cast out Satan? 24 If a kingdom is divided against itself, that kingdom cannot stand. 25 And if a house is divided against itself, that house will not be able to stand. 26 And if Satan has risen up against himself and is divided, he cannot stand, but his end has come. 27 But no one can enter a strong man's house and plunder his property without first tying up the strong man; then indeed the house can be plundered.
> 
> 28 "Truly I tell you, people will be forgiven for their sins and whatever blasphemies they utter; 29 but whoever blasphemes against the Holy Spirit can never have forgiveness, but is guilty of an eternal sin"—30 for they had said, "He has an unclean spirit."

The scribes from Jerusalem accuse Jesus of serving the power of Beelzebub (v. 22). Beelzebub is a god worshipped by a rival group of the Israelites called the Philistines. In 2 Kings 1:2–16 there is a story of the prophet Elijah going to meet messengers of King Ahaziah of Samaria who is in need of healing. Ahaziah inquired for healing from Beelzebub. Elijah tells the messengers that the king will die if he depends on healing from Beelzebub. The

Israelites referred to Beelzebub as "the lord of dung"—a worthless god in their eyes.[2]

Jesus responds to the divide-and-conquer tactics of the scribes by naming the false division they have constructed and asks "How can Satan cast out Satan?"—"If a kingdom is divided against itself, that kingdom cannot stand," and "a house divided against itself cannot stand" (vs. 23-25). Note the progression from the cosmic Satan to the human reign of a kingdom to a house—the very community of the Israelites. In verse 23 we are told Jesus' response is that of parable. In his book *In Parables: The Challenge of the Historical Jesus*, John Dominic Crossan points out the power of the parable as an indictment against the existing social order.[3] Jesus uses parable to indict the scribes' use of mimetic rivalry and to expose the utter meaninglessness of their charges that he is serving the worthless god Beelzebub.

I am looking at this passage within the context of American culture where race, religion, education, gender, sexual orientation, class, ethnicity, and the environment are all issues that can serve to divide the public against itself. In our context the power of the media feeds us images that turn us against one another with news that constructs for us "the situation" that manipulates the story. From an evolutionary point of view this is problematic because our minds are not equipped to distinguish between natural images and those that are artificially created and implanted.[4]

It is worth our attention to note the power of parable used by Jesus as an example for us to follow through our challenging and questioning of the images and "situations" that our media constructs and feeds us. In America we live within our own cultural mythology largely constructed through the media by a tiny minority of wealthy people.[5] Note today the amount of religious programming on TV that promotes self-gain and wealth, while also keeping people in fear through violent end-time apocalyptic

2. Efird, in Achtemeir, et al, eds., *Harper's Bible Dictionary*, 86.
3. Crossan, *In Parables*, 57.
4. Mander, *Four Arguments*, 216-7.
5. Ibid., 143-5.

themes and stories. You will not find an emphasis on Jesus' use of parable to deconstruct the dominant powers of the culture. Yet according to John Dominic Crossan, parable is the main construct of Jesus' message and identity.[6]

Jesus ends his use of parable by saying people will be forgiven every form of blaspheme except the one uttered against the Holy Spirit (v. 29). For Jesus, the Holy Spirit has the power to break free of the blinding power of human mimetic rivalry and its divide and conquer strategies. To refuse the Holy Spirit is to abandon oneself to the blinding power of rivalry that is destined to be destructive. The scribes accuse Jesus of an unclean spirit. Jesus indicts them for abandoning the Holy Spirit (v. 30).

We live in the age of globalization where multinational corporate power brings with it the culture that serves best its bottom line of profiteering and the exploitation of human labor and natural resources. We have shifted from a time of rivalry and division between nations to that of civil conflict and rivalry among citizens within our own communities. Political forces funded by corporate interests make guns ever more available to the public. Deaths by shooting are almost becoming commonplace. The military industrial complex manages to somehow lose American weapons to the latest group of terrorists whom we are told are now among us. Now we are the enemy. Meanwhile the entertainment industry feeds us more violence. The system we are in directs us into violence and death among ourselves, so as to keep our focus off the power that is over us.

Jesus' power of healing threatened the system of religious leadership of his own people. Today, democracy and forces of social justice and human rights are a threat to the multinational corporate system of business. Their fear of taxation is projected into the minds of citizens through the media. We are told we are too poor to support our infrastructures of education, health care, and transportation through taxes. Yet, we are never too poor for more military spending to support their interests even if it means the brewing of civil conflict and war to keep their monopolies

---

6. See Crossan, *The Power of Parable*.

intact. Jesus' use of parable opens for us a narrative that can empower us to unmask the game of divide and conquer that is being played against us. Jesus would go on healing. The narrative of the gospel calls us to go on living and working for the common good, refusing to be divided by powers of special interests whose main purpose is self-serving.

# Luke 5

15 But now more than ever the word about Jesus spread abroad; many crowds would gather to hear him and to be cured of their diseases. 16 But he would withdraw to deserted places and pray.

Luke 6:12 Now during those days he went out to the mountain to pray; and he spent the night in prayer to God.

Mark 6:46 After saying farewell to them, he went up on the mountain to pray.

Luke 12:56 You hypocrites! You know how to interpret the appearance of earth and sky, but why do you not know how to interpret the present time?

There is a moment of innocence and *kairos* (time), when action makes a great deal of sense. But who can recognize such moments? Not one who is debauched by a series of programs. And when all has become absurd, shall one continue to act simply because once, long ago, it made a great deal of sense? As if one were always getting somewhere? There is a time to listen, in the active life and everywhere else, and the better part of action is waiting, not knowing what next, and not having a glib answer.[1]

PRAYER IS AN ESSENTIAL part of the ministry of Jesus for it is the space in which he maintains his relationship to the people he is serving. Thomas Merton, a contemplative monk discovered this about solitude—that it was the place of seeing the social dimension

---

1. Merton, *Conjectures of a Guilty Bystander*, 156.

of our lives, a space to discern what is taking place and how one has been a part of it all. Henri Nouwen followed in the footsteps of Thomas Merton and also noted the dynamics of prayer as solitude. Prayer is essential for our sanity in a divide and conquer world for solitude moves us from sarcasm to contemplation. It moves us from contempt toward the world to compassion.[2] Prayer helps us unmask the illusions, misdirection, disguises, misinformation, and deceit in a culture filled with propaganda from the media.

I have placed the above verse of Luke 12:56 into the context of prayer as an illustration as to why Jesus knows "the time" (the situation and context of events) but his adversaries do not know how to interpret what is taking place. "Time" is perhaps one of the most misinterpreted words in the bible. Biblical Greek uses two words for "time": *kronos,* a length or duration of time; and *kairos,* a quality of time for the in-breaking of God's reign of truth, social justice, and peace. Jesus prays—he enters solitude so as not to let his ego overpower his mission. Prayer is *kairos* time, a space that unmasks the violence of our own mimetic-driven humanity and its rivalries. Prayer as *kairos* is the source for Jesus to speak in parable for it is the place that a counter narrative to the world's powers of oppression and exploitation is conceived. Thus in the gospel we find a dialectical movement of Jesus from proclaiming God's reign/actions of healing and feeding to prayer and onto proclaiming God's reign/actions through more healing and feeding.

James Alison argues that what is taking place in *kairos* time is that the violent apocalyptic end time (*kronos*) scheme of our human mimetic rivalry is being replaced by our being created anew in Jesus Christ.[3] Thus prayer is the means of "stepping out" of the violent schemes of our world and into solitude. Prayer is the space where we discern and discover our call to serve one another and to be stewards of the created order around us. Prayer is the space to recover from our evolutionary mimetic blindness—the lies, disguise, misdirection, and deceit of the marketplace that depends on our conflict and violence for its monopoly of power. It

2. Nouwen, *Thomas Merton.*
3. See Alison, *Living in the End Times.*

is no wonder that Paul once wrote early on in his ministry in 1 Thessalonians 5:17, "pray without ceasing."

# Philippians 2

> 5 Let the same mind be in you that was in Christ Jesus, 6 who, though he was in the form of God, did not regard equality with God as something to be exploited, 7 but emptied himself, taking the form of a slave, being born in human likeness. And being found in human form, 8 he humbled himself and became obedient to the point of death—even death on a cross. 9 Therefore God also highly exalted him and gave him the name that is above every name, 10 so that at the name of Jesus every knee should bend, in heaven and on earth and under the earth, 11 and every tongue should confess that Jesus Christ is Lord, to the glory of God the Father.

THIS PASSAGE IS KNOWN as "the Christ Hymn" and is attributed to Paul. The servant song of Isaiah 53 is likely to be the Hebrew source for the writing of this passage. My interest in this hymn stems from an observation made by Morna D. Hooker that illustrates the dynamics in verses 6 and 7 that relate directly to mimesis, that of not regarding equality with God (not grasping at power) and emptying himself.[1] As mimetic creatures we grasp at others and at the world around us to learn and to grow our identity even to the extent that we aspire to be our own gods. Christ is an anti-mimetic figure who does "not regard equality with God," rather he "empties himself." The word for "empties" is *kenosis* in biblical Greek and it can also be translated as "pours out" (himself).

Martin Luther saw in this passage not only the "emptying" of Christ's life on the cross, but understood *kenosis* as emptying taking place throughout the earthly life of Jesus' ministry.[2] Luther

---

1. Hooker, "The Letter to the Philippians," 506.
2. Althaus, *The Theology of Martin Luther*, 194–8.

saw the incarnation (the Word made flesh in Jesus) as part of the ongoing *kenosis* in the life, death, and resurrection of Jesus Christ. What comes to mind are the words of John Shea whom I heard speak on several occasions as he remarked "By the time they came to take Jesus' life away it was too late for he had already given it away." In our mimetic rivalry we are grasping at saving our own life. In Christ we discover that life is flowing into us and out of us and our identity is no longer that of a mere alienated individual. *Kenosis* is like the understanding of karma that singer/songwriter Willie Nelson writes about. "You get what you give." Willie's good friend Fred Foster said, "The only thing you get to keep in this life is what you gave away."[3] Paul Althaus observed that in Luther's understanding of Jesus Christ deity and humanity are inseparably united.[4] *Kenosis* is the living Word given to us in Jesus Christ that unmasks our mimetic rivalry and violence on the cross and freely offers us identity beyond ourselves in one another. The word for this free offer to live in Christ is *grace*—to live in the flow of kenosis. *Kenosis* is the heart of the salvation story in Jesus Christ.

---

3. Nelson, *Roll Me Up and Smoke Me When I Die*, 72–73.
4. Althaus, *The Theology of Martin Luther*, 198.

# Mark 6

30 The apostles gathered around Jesus, and told him all that they had done and taught. 31 He said to them, "Come away to a deserted place all by yourselves and rest a while." For many were coming and going, and they had no leisure even to eat. 32 And they went away in the boat to a deserted place by themselves. 33 Now many saw them going and recognized them, and they hurried there on foot from all the towns and arrived ahead of them. 34 As he went ashore, he saw a great crowd; and he had compassion for them, because they were like sheep without a shepherd; and he began to teach them many things. 35 When it grew late, his disciples came to him and said, "This is a deserted place, and the hour is now very late; 36 send them away so that they may go into the surrounding country and villages and buy something for themselves to eat." 37 But he answered them, "You give them something to eat." They said to him, "Are we to go and buy two hundred denarii worth of bread, and give it to them to eat?" 38 And he said to them, "How many loaves have you? Go and see." When they had found out, they said, "Five, and two fish." 39 Then he ordered them to get all the people to sit down in groups on the green grass. 40 So they sat down in groups of hundreds and of fifties. 41 Taking the five loaves and the two fish, he looked up to heaven, and blessed and broke the loaves, and gave them to his disciples to set before the people; and he divided the two fish among them all. 42 And all ate and were filled; 43 and they took up twelve baskets full of broken pieces and of the fish. 44 Those who had eaten the loaves numbered five thousand men.

## Salvation Story

THERE ARE SEVERAL WORDS in this story worth noting in order for us to see how Jesus performs *kenosis* in the feeding of five thousand people. The first is the Greek word for "desert"—*eremon*—which has been translated as "deserted place" (vs. 32 and 35). Recall that this is also the description of Jesus' place of solitude and prayer. The Greek word for "compassion" is *esplagnisthay*, which denotes a movement going out from within oneself deeper than one's heart, from one's very bowels (v. 34). The imagery in the story has the crowd going out, arriving ahead of Jesus into a deserted place. Upon seeing the crowd Jesus is going out of himself to minister to them. The disciples have yet to catch up to this movement.

John Shea has written the following about compassion:

> . . . compassion is rooted in the felt perception of solidarity. It is the attitude of people who understand that, despite all that separates us, the last truth is a common humanity within a common Mystery. Compassion is the way into the lives of others to understand their claims and shape our social and political institutions to respond to them. This sense of solidarity is grounded in the valuation of life.[1]

Jesus is going out of himself to the crowd for he sees that they are "like sheep without a shepherd" (v. 34). This is commentary on the religious leaders of Jesus' time, whose allegiance to the Roman Empire results in their safe operation of religion that does not challenge the status quo, and therefore does not serve the people. Regarding our own time, Robin Meyers writes, "What most people do not realize is that the church has become a stepchild of the Empire. It has lost the independent voice it needs."[2] Into this void left by the religious leaders, Jesus teaches them many things (v. 34).

In contrast to Jesus, whose attention is entirely focused on the crowd of people, the disciples' attention is on the time of day being late and the lack of food resources in a deserted place. Scarcity is the worldview of the disciples. Scarcity is the view of people who feel disempowered. Scarcity is what the Empire uses

---

1. Shea, *Stories of God*, 114.
2. Meyers, *The Underground Church*, 92.

to control people. Today it is called austerity. The disciples want to send the people away to the marketplace for food. But Jesus' life is rooted in *kenosis* and compassion and therefore he sees the life of the people, not the marketplace, as the primary resource at hand. Jesus responds "You give them something to eat" (v. 37). The disciples are still in the mindset of the marketplace and the Empire and begin figuring the great cost that it would take to feed so many people. In v. 38 Jesus asks, "How many loaves have you? Go and see." In Greek both *go* and *see* are in the imperative and should be read with an exclamation point.

The disciples have been blind up until this point to any potential resources among themselves. They are focused on their hunger and separated it from the hunger of the crowd, which is more than mere hunger for food, but also hunger for the nourishment of teaching that Jesus is offering with his very words. John Shea once remarked, "You are only in a desolate place as long as you do not know what you have." The mindset of scarcity is to see nothing. As it turns out the disciples have five loaves of bread and two fish (v. 38).

Jesus has the people sit in groups on the grass (vs. 39–40). They are grouped as Jesus is with his disciples. Here is mimesis—copying the action of Jesus and his disciples. The next important word and action in the story is "blessing," *eulogayson* (v. 41). Jesus blesses the bread and fish; he looks up to heaven and acknowledges its true source, God. Blessing is a word that is perverted by prosperity preachers in today's media who place emphasis on its meaning as getting material things and financial resources for oneself. The entire context of blessing with Jesus is the action of teaching, breaking bread and sharing fish, feeding the people's hunger for truth and their physical hunger. "Blessing" for Jesus is an act of total solidarity of his life going out to all of the people gathered. Blessing is the action that sets *kenosis* in motion as the sharing of our life and our resources with others.

The story concludes with all being filled (v. 42). Twelve baskets are left—one for each disciple. They who saw too little also receive a lesson from Jesus through discovering too much (v. 43).

Then we receive the final punch line—five thousand are fed (v. 44). From the standpoint of human mimesis Jesus breaks through the myth of scarcity that disempowers people and is often the source of their violence.[3] The crowd saw and followed Jesus past the blindness of his disciples. Blessing set *kenosis* in action among them all, starting with Jesus as its source.

---

3. Schwartz, *The Curse of Cain*, 83.

# Mark 10

17 As he was setting out on a journey, a man ran up and knelt before him, and asked him, "Good Teacher, what must I do to inherit eternal life?" 18 Jesus said to him, "Why do you call me good? No one is good but God alone. 19 You know the commandments: 'You shall not murder; You shall not commit adultery; You shall not steal; You shall not bear false witness; You shall not defraud; Honor your father and mother.'" 20 He said to him, "Teacher, I have kept all these since my youth." 21 Jesus, looking at him, loved him and said, "You lack one thing; go, sell what you own, and give the money to the poor, and you will have treasure in heaven; then come, follow me." 22 When he heard this, he was shocked and went away grieving, for he had many possessions. 23 Then Jesus looked around and said to his disciples, "How hard it will be for those who have wealth to enter the kingdom of God!" 24 And the disciples were perplexed at these words. But Jesus said to them again, "Children, how hard it is to enter the kingdom of God! 25 It is easier for a camel to go through the eye of a needle than for someone who is rich to enter the kingdom of God." 26 They were greatly astounded and said to one another, "Then who can be saved?" 27 Jesus looked at them and said, "For mortals it is impossible, but not for God; for God all things are possible."

WHEN JESUS IS APPROACHED by a man addressing him as "good teacher," the encounter becomes the occasion for Jesus to teach that humans are not "good," God alone is good (v. 18). The teaching continues with Jesus reeling off the Fourth through Tenth Commandments in verse 19 (see Exodus 20:1–7; Deuteronomy 5:1–21). The man is quick to reply that he has kept all of these since his youth (v. 20). There is a bit of humor tucked into this reply and the editorial title given to this passage in bibles where it is titled "The Rich Young Man." A person with any real amount of life experience has broken any number of these commandments. Thus, this guy must indeed really be "young."

Missing from the list of commandments that Jesus gives the man are the First, Second, and Third Commandments, the ones that cover human relationship with God. The lesson unfolds in the following verses. Jesus looks at him and "loved him" (v. 21). Love is translated from the Greek *agapé* and here it is in the indicative voice, making it the subject matter at hand. *Agapé* is love that is willing to give of oneself for one's neighbor; it is rooted in the *kenosis* of Jesus' way of living. The question at hand is to "inherit eternal life." One does not earn an inheritance; one receives it as gift. Having received it as gift empowers one to give one's life to others. It is God who establishes relationship with us, not through our grasping and working. Here, Jesus is trying to establish relationship between this man and the people that Jesus serves. Thus the final instruction from Jesus to the man becomes to sell what he has, give the money to the poor, resulting in having reward in heaven and following him (v. 21). The man is shocked, goes away grieving, for he has many possessions (v. 22). Jesus continues to teach and now addresses his disciples, telling them it is difficult for the wealthy to enter the kingdom of God (v. 23). Jesus comes back to relationship with God and the commandments missing from those kept by the wealthy man.

It is a common misconception that Christianity is based on morals. Instead, it is based on relationship with God through Jesus Christ and no mere morals. The man is missing a relationship with God, and therefore relationship with neighbor. His wealth is standing in the way. Luther, writing on the First Commandment once said, "Many a person thinks they have God and entire sufficiency if they have money and riches and securely boast that they care for no one . . . This is a universal idol upon earth."[1] Following the work of Luther, Paul Althaus writes:

1. Luther, *Large Catechism*, 11.

Moralism is regarded as idolatry and blasphemy . . . The way of moralism is not only an ethical illusion, since no (one) can keep the commandments; it is primarily a religious fiction, because the God with whom one thinks [they] are dealing in this way is nothing but a figure of the imagination of one's own heart.[2]

In verse 25, Jesus illustrates the impossibility of holding onto one's wealth and entering the kingdom of God with the illustration of a camel trying to pass through the eye of a (sewing) needle. I have often heard the apologetic explanation that this "needle" Jesus was referring to was a thin opening in the wall around Jerusalem that camels had to kneel down and crawl through. Yet, there is no evidence that the text is referring to a narrow gate in the walls of Jerusalem.[3]

Our reading of the literary context shows us that the man grasping for moral goodness has missed how Jesus omitted the first three commandments only to learn the very first commandment cannot be followed by holding onto his wealth. It is impossible to follow Jesus by one's own power and wealth. The disciples' response confirms this in their question of "then who can be saved?" (v. 26). Jesus' response sums it up. Human power cannot do it. With God all things are possible (v. 27).

Pope Francis has addressed the issue of the concentration of wealth and power in relationship to care for the environment. According to the pope, any true ecological debate must bring together "both the cry of the earth and the cry of the poor."[4] Francis observes how multinational businesses leave behind environmental liabilities around the world, while also using debt to control nations and their people.[5] The observations of Pope Francis find support in the work of journalist Naomi Klein in *The Shock Doctrine: The Rise of Disaster Capitalism*. The predominant political powers of our time are practicing "free-market fundamentalism"

---

2. Althaus, *The Theology of Martin Luther*, 126.
3. Achtemeier, et al, *Harper's Dictionary of the Bible*, 692.
4. The Holy See, *On Care for Our Common Home*, point 49.
5. Ibid., points 51 and 52.

that rejects all things public and governmental in order to move public money into the hands of private corporate power.[6] These riches are what grieve the man in our story for they are the ultimate idol he worships and follows. Unless he lets go of his idolatry the rich man cannot follow Jesus.

In his book *One Nation under God: How Corporate America Invented Christian America*, Kevin M. Kruse shows that it was business interests that introduced god-language into the pledge of allegiance as a move against the social programs of President Roosevelt's New Deal which addressed the economic needs of Americans during the Great Depression.[7] As we saw earlier in the work of Karen Armstrong, secular powers use religion for their agendas. I maintain that Christianity is not a religion. What we find today in America is the making of Christianity into religion, so as to remove its power for exposing human greed, violence, and corruption. By making Christianity back into religion the multinational corporate power of our era essentially perverts the gospel back into the ancient mythology rooted in violence and death. However, it is my claim that to do so they must avoid any serious reading of the texts of scripture, especially a reading of the text from the perspective of the cross of Jesus.

In his book *Wait Without Idols*, Gabriel Vahanian argues that in biblical thought "goodness is not quantitative, but always a relational quality."[8] The rich man replies "I have kept all these" (commandments). But the commandments that address our idolatry, which keep us out of relationship with a God who is incarnate in our neighbor, are missing. And the disciples' question is on point: "then who can be saved?" For this relationship is being initiated by one who loves us despite our idolatry. Jesus looked upon the rich man with love—*agapé*. Jesus would not let the rich man's idolatry go unchecked. But more so, Jesus pours out the remainder of his life on a cross, not as some payment sacrifice for our sin to a violent god, but as a final act to expose once and for all our violent human

---

6. Klein, *The Shock Doctrine*, 446–9.
7 See Kruse, *One Nation Under God*.
8. Vahanian, *Wait Without Idols*, 134.

mimetic rivalry and our need for an identity in a God invested in and living in our humanity. It is with this God that all things are possible for us. To see such a God, we must look from the cross of Jesus Christ. It is from the perspective of the cross that we see the two-fold dynamic of *the salvation story*—the final exposure of our human game of mimesis and the offer of new life in the risen Christ. It is this dynamic that Martin Luther captured about the cross that makes a Christian free to live in relationship with the world.

> A Christian is the most free lord of all, subject to none.
>
> A Christian is the most dutiful servant of all; subject to everyone.[9]

---

9. Ibid., 181.

# Luke 23

1 Then the assembly rose as a body and brought Jesus before Pilate. 2 They began to accuse him, saying, "We found this man perverting our nation, forbidding us to pay taxes to the emperor, and saying that he himself is the Messiah, a king." 3 Then Pilate asked him, "Are you the king of the Jews?" He answered, "You say so." 4 Then Pilate said to the chief priests and the crowds, "I find no basis for an accusation against this man." 5 But they were insistent and said, "He stirs up the people by teaching throughout all Judea, from Galilee where he began even to this place." 6 When Pilate heard this, he asked whether the man was a Galilean. 7 And when he learned that he was under Herod's jurisdiction, he sent him off to Herod, who was himself in Jerusalem at that time. 8 When Herod saw Jesus, he was very glad, for he had been wanting to see him for a long time, because he had heard about him and was hoping to see him perform some sign. 9 He questioned him at some length, but Jesus gave him no answer. 10 The chief priests and the scribes stood by, vehemently accusing him. 11 Even Herod with his soldiers treated him with contempt and mocked him; then he put an elegant robe on him, and sent him back to Pilate. 12 That same day Herod and Pilate became friends with each other; before this they had been enemies.

First there are the religious leaders, then the politicians, and above all the crowd. They all participate in the action—at first separately, but gradually more and more in unison. Note that all these forces intervene in the order of their importance, beginning with the weakest and ending with the strongest . . . Pilate is the person with real power, but ahead of him is the crowd. Once mobilized, the crowd has absolute power, dragging institutions with

## Luke 23

> it . . . Pilate's decision is too easy, actually, to illustrate clearly the subordination of the ruler to the crowd and the dominant role of the crowd at the moment of greatest excitement when the mechanism of the scapegoat is set in motion.[1]

WE BEGAN THE EXPLORATION of mimesis in the scriptures with the story of 1 Samuel 8 and the people of Israel wanting a king. Here the religious leaders and crowds are making Jesus into a rival king to the Roman Empire. Here we can see that scripture is uncovering the ancient ritual of sacrificing the tribal king with a substitute—a scapegoat. For example, in Joseph Campbell's treatment of *The King, and the Virgin of the Vestal Fire,* the king is killed every seven years and sooner if the crops fail.[2] Here Jesus, not Herod, not Pilate, will be killed. In these texts of scripture, the dynamics of mimetic rivalry are on display and not concealed.

According to Girard the mimetic reading of the gospel essentially opens up to us the world of violence and evil. The same force that divides us cannot also unite us against a common *scapegoat* that is innocent.[3] At the end of the Luke 23 passage, we find that Pilate and Herod, two previous enemies, are now united as friends (v. 12). According to Girard, by putting Jesus to death, the powers of death have fallen into a trap and have been exposed.[4] Myths are incapable of disclosing to us the inner working of our human violence. "Only a mimetic reading"[5] of these texts can reveal the human scapegoat mechanism.

By and large people in American culture who identify themselves as Christians *do not* read scripture from a mimetic standpoint. By and large American Christians read the scriptures, in particular the death of Jesus, from the standpoint that evolved from the writings of St. Anselm of Canterbury. According to

---

1. Girard, *The Scapegoat*, 105–6.
2. Campbell, *Primitive Mythology*, 165–9.
3. Girard, *The Scapegoat*, 195–6.
4. Ibid., 108.
5. Girard, *The One by Whom Scandal Comes*, 36–37.

Anselm's writing titled *Why God Became Man,* human sin had offended God's honor. Man owed something back to God in order to restore this honor. Since humans, who are sinners, are incapable of repaying God to restore God's honor, only Jesus could supply the payment through his death.[6] Anselm's interpretation of the death of Jesus essentially reads scripture through the lens of mythology, thus restoring the violent gods of ancient battle myths. Anselm's rendering of the death of Jesus masks the violent mimetic scapegoating of humans. Anselm's reading of Jesus' death is at the root of why so many Americans who call themselves Christian cannot see their complicity in the power of violence at work within themselves, their churches, and their culture: they see that payment for their sin has been made instead of seeing violent mimetic rivalry at work and turning from sin to new life in Jesus Christ.

According to James Alison, what is taking place in a mimetic reading of the death of Jesus is that now God is worshipped, not through the exclusion of the victim or over and against a victim, but rather *from* the perspective of the victim. Alison writes,

> What is offered is the possibility for humans to form a new society which does not need victims or exclusions in order for its sense of identity to be built up. This is not because everyone is suddenly good, or nice. Rather it is because the victim is given us: God has provided for sacrifice. So, membership of this new Israel involves a new way of relating to the victim. It involves the unlearning of all those patterns of behavior which depend on, or tend to produce, victims. Simultaneously, it involves learning how to relate to, side with, stand up for those who are cast out, excluded and so on. It involves living for others in such a way that those doing so are always prepared to run the risk of expulsion and exclusion themselves rather than basing their security on expelling and excluding others. This is bearing witness to the truth which comes from the victim. The Greek word for witness is the word which gives us our word 'martyr'.[7]

6. Davies and Evans, *Anselm of Canterbury,* 260–356.
7. Alison, *Knowing Jesus,* 72–73.

## Luke 23

The issue of our identity is at the center of *the salvation story*. By nature we are forming our identity out of rivalry, violence, and scapegoats. Mythology and religion are our hiding of this phenomenon. It is a mimetic reading of scripture that reveals this scheme and offers us a way out. Our identity with the one who has died—Jesus Christ—makes us witnesses of this story known as the gospel. This places our self at risk. Only faith in our life being made alive in all others joined to this One who lives in all can be our source of hope and love.

> Luke 23:33 When they came to the place that is called The Skull, they crucified Jesus there with the criminals, one on his right and one on his left. 34 Then Jesus said, "Father, forgive them; for they do not know what they are doing." And they cast lots to divide his clothing. 35 And the people stood by, watching; but the leaders scoffed at him, saying, "He saved others; let him save himself if he is the Messiah of God, his chosen one!" 36 The soldiers also mocked him, coming up and offering him sour wine, 37 and saying, "If you are the King of the Jews, save yourself!" 38 There was also an inscription over him, "This is the King of the Jews." 39 One of the criminals who were hanged there kept deriding him and saying, "Are you not the Messiah? Save yourself and us!" 40 But the other rebuked him, saying, "Do you not fear God, since you are under the same sentence of condemnation? 41 And we indeed have been condemned justly, for we are getting what we deserve for our deeds, but this man has done nothing wrong." 42 Then he said, "Jesus, remember me when you come into your kingdom." 43 He replied, "Truly I tell you, today you will be with me in Paradise."

The crucifixion of Jesus is proof that it was indeed Pilate the Roman procurator who handed on this sentence, for he was the only one with such authority. Second, it affirms that the charge given Jesus was high treason for being a rival king to Caesar's sovereignty. The placing of a placard for their crime was also a common part of the ordeal.[8] We find reference to such an inscription in verse 38.

We have already established the blind mimetic rivalry of the mob that manipulated Pilate into carrying out this sentence. Luke gives us the continued dynamic of opposing views in two thieves who are crucified along with Jesus (v. 33). Before any of the scoffing and rivalry can be heard from the bystanders and soldiers, Luke gives us the words of forgiveness from Jesus (v. 34). According to Girard, what is taking place on the cross is that God is using the scapegoat mechanism at God's own expense in order to subvert it.[9] Through the cross God exposes the blind violence of our mimetic rivalry and we are forgiven in order to turn and live anew out of the identity offered to us in Jesus Christ. The implications of Jesus' offer of forgiveness destroy the rivalry in this scene. It means that all the scoffers including the one criminal on the cross next to Jesus are forgiven. This is in keeping with what Girard has noted: "divine power is not destructive; it does not expel anyone."[10]

Verses 40–43 provide us with the exchange between the other criminal and Jesus in which we hear Jesus declared to be innocent (v. 41). Thus the death of Jesus reveals the breakdown of justice in humans due to mimetic rivalry. From a theological perspective and a literary perspective this prisoner is now able to see the scapegoat mechanism. It has been revealed to him because Jesus has already pronounced forgiveness, which he has received and therefore is now able to see, no longer being mimetically blind like the others. The criminal then asks to be remembered in Jesus' kingdom. Here we find the ability to indeed see Jesus' kingship as being part of life out of death beyond the powers of human empires and their violence. In verse 43 Jesus affirms the request of the criminal.

Gerhard O. Forde has written a book titled *Justification by Faith: A Matter of Death and Life*. In it Forde argues that what is taking place in the death and resurrection of Jesus is not merely

---

8. Bassler, in Achtemeir, et al, eds., *Harper's Dictionary of the Bible*, 194.
9. Girard, *The One by Whom Scandal Comes*, 43.
10. Girard, *The Scapegoat*, 191.

life after death, but rather life out of death.[11] In the Girardian framework, mimetic rivalry must die in us before we can be remembered. Otherwise the rivalry walls us from one another. In forgiveness the mimetic wall is destroyed, and the life of the other is able to be remembered by us and live in us. The Gospel of Luke gives us a complete introduction to the dynamics of life out of the death of mimetic rivalry in its most gruesome of scenes—the crucifixion of Jesus Christ, one who is innocent yet forgives. Our mimetic humanity has no capacity for its own righteousness. In the cross of Jesus Christ, God has come to us to expose our violence, pronounce forgiveness, and empower us to remember and be remembered in life that is now set free from the power of death that we make by our own mimesis.

---

11. Forde, *Justification by Faith*, 15–19.

# John 20

1 Early on the first day of the week, while it was still dark, Mary Magdalene came to the tomb and saw that the stone had been removed from the tomb. 2 So she ran and went to Simon Peter and the other disciple, the one whom Jesus loved, and said to them, "They have taken the Lord out of the tomb, and we do not know where they have laid him." 3 Then Peter and the other disciple set out and went toward the tomb. 4 The two were running together, but the other disciple outran Peter and reached the tomb first. 5 He bent down to look in and saw the linen wrappings lying there, but he did not go in. 6 Then Simon Peter came, following him, and went into the tomb. He saw the linen wrappings lying there, 7 and the cloth that had been on Jesus' head, not lying with the linen wrappings but rolled up in a place by itself. 8 Then the other disciple, who reached the tomb first, also went in, and he saw and believed; 9 for as yet they did not understand the scripture, that he must rise from the dead. 10 Then the disciples returned to their homes.

JOHN'S GOSPEL EMPLOYS THE use of double entendre—double meaning. Mary Magdalene goes to the tomb of Jesus "while it was still dark" (v. 1). Then we receive the story of an empty tomb reported by Mary who runs to the disciples Simon Peter and "the one whom Jesus loved" (most likely John) in verses 2–4, and a foot race between them to the empty tomb. We receive only the report of Jesus' wrappings lying there and a detail of a cloth from Jesus' head rolled up in a place by itself (v. 7). Some commentaries see the neatly placed cloths as a defense against the idea that Jesus' body has been taken by grave robbers, since robbers would not take the

## JOHN 20

time to neatly roll up the wrappings.[1] I think John is showing us that when the disciples do not understand the scripture; all they have is the mundane details and nothing more. They are indeed "in the dark" regarding what happened to the body of Jesus, for verse 9 informs us that "they did not understand the scripture, that he must rise from the dead." The disciples return to their homes—plural—as if to say their excitement is over, they parted ways, and life for them is "back to normal."

This scene brings to mind the work of John Douglas Hall's *Waiting for Gospel*, where Hall calls for an understanding of the bible beyond literalism and fundamentalism.[2] The above passage leaves us literally with nothing to report of interest beyond physical details of an empty tomb and Jesus' linen wrappings. Girard complains that without a mimetic view of the events we are left with "a thousand ways to avoid the understanding of the Gospels."[3] According to Girard's mimetic reading of John, this gospel account rejects the triumph of human violence. The *logos*—the Word that created life—also creates life out of death, instead of life ordered around human violence and the hiding of all the evidence of its murderous ways.[4]

As long as the church and those who identify themselves as "Christians" are lost in the physical details of the resurrection, as the two male disciples in the above passage are, we will indeed remain in the dark about the meaning of the gospel. Dietrich Bonhoeffer who in his final days while in prison for opposing the German Nazi regime, wrote in his *Letters and Papers from Prison* that the church is only the church when it exists for others. This means that the church shares in the problems of the secular world and must turn from the worship of power, for to live in Christ is to live for others.[5] Simon Peter and the beloved disciple have returned to their homes. But soon they will be turned outward to live for

---

1. See O'Day, "The Gospel of John," 841.
2. Hall, *Waiting for Gospel*, 14.
3. Girard, *The Scapegoat*, 109.
4. Girard, *Things Hidden Since the Foundation of the World*, 270–80.
5. Bonhoeffer, *Letters and Papers*, 211.

others, for Mary Magdalene is still back at the tomb and this scene is not by any means over.

> John 20:11 But Mary stood weeping outside the tomb. As she wept, she bent over to look into the tomb; 12 and she saw two angels in white, sitting where the body of Jesus had been lying, one at the head and the other at the feet. 13 They said to her, "Woman, why are you weeping?" She said to them, "They have taken away my Lord, and I do not know where they have laid him." 14 When she had said this, she turned around and saw Jesus standing there, but she did not know that it was Jesus. 15 Jesus said to her, "Woman, why are you weeping? Whom are you looking for?" Supposing him to be the gardener, she said to him, "Sir, if you have carried him away, tell me where you have laid him, and I will take him away." 16 Jesus said to her, "Mary!" She turned and said to him in Hebrew, "Rabbouni!" (which means Teacher). 17 Jesus said to her, "Do not hold on to me, because I have not yet ascended to the Father. But go to my brothers and say to them, 'I am ascending to my Father and your Father, to my God and your God.'" 18 Mary Magdalene went and announced to the disciples, "I have seen the Lord"; and she told them that he had said these things to her.

Mary is outside the tomb of Jesus weeping (v. 11). The Greek verb is *klaiousa;* it is in the present active tense and in the nominative case to denote the main subject—grief. Grief is formed by what is missing and absent in one's life. Note how Mary's experience is totally shaped by a different lens than the other two disciples who visited the tomb. Whereas the other two male disciples make mere physical observations and show no emotion of loss, Mary is in a state of grief looking for where people have taken the body of Jesus. From a mimetic standpoint, Mary does not copy the disciples and leave the tomb. Mary attends to her grief and looks into the tomb for herself. She sees two angels—*angelos* is Greek for "messenger," (v. 12). John's gospel only makes one other mention of angels in 1:51, and this is in reference to the call of Jesus' disciple Nathaniel who someday will see greater things in the opening of

## JOHN 20

the heavens and ascending and descending of angels, namely his resurrection. "White" is the image of baptismal robes that stand for the life of believers in Jesus Christ and is referenced mostly in another work attributed to John, the book of Revelation.

> Revelation 7:13 Then one of the elders addressed me, saying, "Who are these, robed in white, and where have they come from?" 14 I said to him, "Sir, you are the one that knows." Then he said to me, "These are they who have come out of the great ordeal; they have washed their robes and made them white in the blood of the Lamb.

The scene is loaded with grief. Mary, too, has been through the ordeal of Jesus' death. Then the angels ask Mary, "Why are you weeping?" Their question breaks into Mary's framing of events, but she persists in knowing where "her Lord" is and insists that he has been taken away (v. 13). For Mary, the grave wrappings neatly ordered mean nothing, she has come to see Jesus and she speaks of him in the possessive: "my Lord." Verses 14 and 15 give us the exchange between Jesus and Mary starting with Jesus repeating the same question of the angels, adding, "Whom are you looking for?" Mary takes Jesus to be the gardener and insinuates that he has carried him away and that if so, he should tell her where he is so that she can take back his body. Paul Ricœur once wrote, "Primitive Christianity never perceived any fundamental difference between the eyewitness testimonies of the life of Jesus and the encounter with the risen Lord."[6] In her grief Mary has broken away from the male disciples' world of mimesis—the one that manages a footrace to the tomb, but is too numb to feel any loss. In her grief Mary is able to experience the life of the risen Jesus in the stranger—one she supposes to be "the gardener." Upon hearing the voice from this "gardener" say "Mary!", she responds with Jesus' title of teacher—"Rabbouni!"

What we have is a lesson on how human grief and loss can open to life beyond mimetic rivalry. Here Jesus is discovered as present in another person who is not the exact object of her desire

---

6. Ricœur, *Essays*, 135.

and loss, yet who can constitute the very presence of "her Lord." Thus in the very next verse, 17, Jesus addresses Mary's desire to "hold onto" him for to do so is an act of her control and grasping (which is at the root of mimetic desire). The risen Lord is not the object of our control and desire. Control and desire is the root of our mimetic rivalry and a return to religion and violence. The risen Lord marks the end of mimetic desire, rivalry, and violence.

Then we receive the language of Jesus saying that he has not yet "ascended to God." This is theological language addressing Jesus' ongoing identity to be revealed as one with God—the main theme of John's gospel. But if we read it like the disciples who went home, who do not yet understand the scriptures, we will read it in physical terms and think Jesus needs to leave the earth and go off to a disconnected "heaven." But angels are present. The heavens are opened. The integral vision of all things becoming one in the risen Lord is unfolding along with the wrappings in the tomb.

The resurrection of Jesus Christ enters into an unlikely and unlikable space of human experience—loss and grief. Mary Magdalene's attending to her grief led to an encounter with the risen Christ. The risen Lord is not to be found in the power of mimetic rivalry. The risen Lord is not understood in disconnected categories of space and physical details that separate heaven and earth. The risen Lord transcends all this, including our separations of "gardener" and "Lord." Mary, having experienced all this, returns to the disciples and announces that she has seen the Lord.

> John 20:19 When it was evening on that day, the first day of the week, and the doors of the house where the disciples had met were locked for fear of the Jews, Jesus came and stood among them and said, "Peace be with you." 20 After he said this, he showed them his hands and his side. Then the disciples rejoiced when they saw the Lord. 21 Jesus said to them again, "Peace be with you. As the Father has sent me, so I send you." 22 When he had said this, he breathed on them and said to them, "Receive the Holy Spirit. 23 If you forgive the sins of any, they are forgiven them; if you retain the sins of any, they are retained."

## JOHN 20

Both appearances of Jesus in John 20 occur in "darkness." The first was in the morning, as darkness also is mentioned in parallel to the disciples' not yet understanding the scriptures. The above passage is now set in the evening and "darkness" is now occurring in the context of the disciples' "fear of the Jews." Darkness in John is more than the absence of physical light; it is also the disciples' inability to see the risen Lord.

Verse 19 discloses to us the entire mimetic issue in the Gospel of John—the division between Jews who followed Jesus and those who did not. John 9:22 and 12:42 both speak of fear in connection with being put out of the synagogue for going against the religious leadership and power of the Pharisees as a result of following Jesus. Now with the death of Jesus the disciples' fear is only heightened as they fear for their own lives. Paul Ricœur writes of how our personhood and identity is essentially the construct of a social narrative built on our past human interactions. This view implies that our identity is not merely held by ourselves but it is also embodied in the lives of others through their memories and their mimetic copying of us.[7] The disciples' fear has shut down their social narrative of Jesus. The images of darkness and locked doors and fear speak to what is keeping the presence of Jesus away from the disciples. Yet the disciples and Jesus himself are all Jews. In reality the disciples are divided against themselves. Into this fear and division, the disciples hear Jesus' greeting of peace. These words represent a "breaking in" of the narrative and identity of Jesus that were foretold in John 16:32–33, to be addressed.

In verse 20 we read how Jesus showed the disciples his hands and side—the wounds from his crucifixion. James Alison writes on how the risen Jesus is not a mere continuation of his former self. Jesus is not life after death. Jesus is life out of death. Jesus comes bearing wounds as one who is both "crucified and risen"—as the one who is always the other—victim of our human violence and simultaneously the one who forgives. The risen Jesus with wounds uncovers the violence we hide in our myths. The risen Jesus

---

7. Ricœur, *Oneself as Another*, 140–168.

empties the power of our mimetic rivalry by refusing retaliation, and returns to the disciples love beyond death.[8]

> John 16:32 The hour is coming, indeed it has come, when you will be scattered, each one to his home, and you will leave me alone. Yet I am not alone because the Father is with me. 33 I have said this to you, so that in me you may have peace. In the world you face persecution. But take courage; I have conquered the world!"

John 16:32 is also uniquely joined to John 20:22 in that these are the only verses in John's gospel that use the verb *aphate*—"to forgive" or "leave." Verse 33 tells us of Jesus' promise of peace that will empower the disciples to take on persecution, knowing that his presence cannot be destroyed by death—the world's power of mimetic rivalry.

Fear has been broken by the presence of Jesus' identity in the midst of the disciples as his narrative and promise of peace is remembered. Here is the resurrection breakthrough—the positive power of mimesis is in the remembering of Jesus and in the following of him despite all the wounds of his crucifixion and death. John joins together the power of forgiveness in Jesus' words of "peace" and his giving to the disciples his Spirit, conferring upon them the very power of forgiveness to exercise in the world. The narrative identity and character of Jesus that was already embodied in the disciples, as well as others, has now been set free to be the presence of the risen Christ for the world.

Let us again make note of that which is not part of the narrative identity of Jesus. There is no reprisal from God for the death of Jesus. The battle myth has been ended. There is *peace* and *forgiveness* in the place of more violence. The positive side of human mimesis has been restored as resurrection marks the realization of our life extending to others and their life extending to us through this event of the risen Christ. In the resurrection of Jesus, the power of fear is broken and continues to be broken wherever and whenever someone experiences the breakthrough of all the lives of

---

8. Alison, *The Joy of Being Wrong*, 75–77.

people whose image and memory provides peace, comfort, direction, wisdom and the courage to live and love. The resurrection is indeed bodily as the life of Jesus comes to be embodied in all of humanity.

# Ephesians

> 2:8 For by grace you have been saved through faith, and this is not your own doing; it is the gift of God—9 not the result of works, so that no one may boast.

IN HER COMMENTARY ON Ephesians, Pheme Perkins notes how this letter is not the work of Paul. In particular, she notes how the subject of "the law" is not referred to in conjunction with the work of God's "grace"—*charis*—gift. Because of grace there is no longer a distinction between Jew and Gentile.[1] Thus the writer of this work continues in verses 15–16:

> 15 He has abolished the law with its commandments and ordinances, that he might create in himself one new humanity in place of the two, thus making peace, 16 and might reconcile both groups to God in one body through the cross, thus putting to death that hostility through it.

The writer of Ephesians captures the power of the death and resurrection of Christ as ending the "hostility" of mimetic rivalry through the power of grace—the gift of forgiveness that restores the life-giving side of mimesis and our true narrative identity in reconciliation with one another. This grace is never our work because it comes in the form of gift from one who is "other"—Christ—who is now present in all of human life.

> Ephesians 4:4 There is one body and one Spirit, just as you were called to the one hope of your calling, 5 one Lord, one faith, one baptism, 6 one God and Father of all, who is above all and through all and in all.

---

1. Perkins, "Ephesians," 356.

Review my earlier commentary on Romans 6 and you will find that the writer of Ephesians has beautifully expounded upon Paul's understanding of baptism. Through the power of grace, God's forgiveness utterly opens our identity beyond our self and extends it to the life not only of all other people, but all of creation itself. As Perkins has noted, the power of God's grace now makes us "a new humanity" joined to the cosmic body of Christ.[2] Grace as forgiveness liberates us from the power of mimetic rivalry and restores the narrative identity of who we are in relationship to all humankind and creation.

> Ephesians 4:7 But each of us was given grace according to the measure of Christ's gift. 8 Therefore it is said, "When he ascended on high he made captivity itself a captive; he gave gifts to his people." 9 (When it says, "He ascended," what does it mean but that he had also descended into the lower parts of the earth? 10 He who descended is the same one who ascended far above all the heavens, so that he might fill all things.)

In verses 7 and 8, grace (the power of God's forgiveness) comes bearing gifts for people. In verse 8 we find the saying about Christ's ascending on high making "captivity a captive." The "ascending on high" is a referral back to the image of the *cross* that Ephesians gives us above in 2:16. The cross has the power to end human hostility. Girard argues that through the cross God reuses the scapegoat mechanism in order to subvert it.[3] Reading with the lens of mimesis we see that "captivity" (the power of mimetic rivalry-division-violence-death) has now been exposed once and for all by the crucifixion of Jesus Christ. The gift of grace-forgiveness frees our humanity from the violent captivity of reprisal as a pathway is now open for us to imitate a non-violent God. Indeed, this positive form of mimesis is the end argument of this ongoing line of thought in Ephesians with the very words "be imitators of God" (5:1).

2. Ibid.
3. Girard, *The One by Whom Scandal Comes*, 43.

Verses 9 and 10 speak of Christ's ascending and descending and having the ability to fill all things. Perkins argues that this is a theme carried forward from Ephesians 1:20–23.[4]

> 20 God put this power to work in Christ when he raised him from the dead and seated him at his right hand in the heavenly places, 21 far above all rule and authority and power and dominion, and above every name that is named, not only in this age but also in the age to come. 22 And he has put all things under his feet and has made him the head over all things for the church, 23 which is his body, the fullness of him who fills all in all.

Perkins also notes how the above passage is based off of Psalm 110. However, there is a striking difference between the images in Psalm 110 and those in Ephesians. In Psalm 110 we find the violent image of God who shatters the power of kings filling people not with gifts, but with corpses.

> Psalm 110:5 The Lord is at your right hand; he will shatter kings on the day of his wrath. 6 He will execute judgment among the nations, filling them with corpses; he will shatter heads over the wide earth.

The cross of Jesus Christ together with the gift of grace-forgiveness has now shattered the power of mimetic rivalry, violence, and death. It is this action of God's grace-forgiveness that is universally available to all people, since all humanity shares in mimesis. Girard's colleague, Jean-Michel Oughourlian argues that we as humans are completely immersed in mimetism.[5] Therefore, from a mimetic perspective, we see by subverting mimetic rivalry, violence, and death, Jesus Christ is indeed the universal presence of God's grace to all. The old in-groups and out-groups are destroyed in God's action through the power of the cross and the resurrection.

> Ephesians 4:11 The gifts he gave were that some would be apostles, some prophets, some evangelists, some pastors

---

4. Perkins, "Ephesians," 421.
5. Girard, *Things Hidden Since the Foundation of the World*, 199.

and teachers, 12 to equip the saints for the work of ministry, for building up the body of Christ, 13 until all of us come to the unity of the faith and of the knowledge of the Son of God, to maturity, to the measure of the full stature of Christ.

In verses 11 and 12 we find that the presence of God's grace comes in the form of a diversity of gifts that empower people to lead for the building up of Christ's body—the new humanity. This *diversity* reflects the positive power of mimesis now released through Christ, as we have seen previously that "likeness" to one another is the source of competition and rivalry. Christ is a process of "maturing," like the God of becoming that we noted back in Exodus 3:14. Note that the end purpose of these gifts is Christ, not the church. Any legitimate purpose of the church can only be grounded in nurturing the diversity of gifts in all people for the end purpose of liberating humanity and creation from the power of mimetic rivalry and destruction.

> Ephesians 4:25 So then, putting away falsehood, let all of us speak the truth to our neighbors, for we are members of one another. 26 Be angry but do not sin; do not let the sun go down on your anger, 27 and do not make room for the devil.

In verse 25 we find that our true existence is as "members of one another." Life in Christ puts away the "falsehood" of individualism. Following the work of Girard, James Alison writes on the dynamics of mimesis that I find applying well to Ephesians. First, the entire creation of who we are depends on the *other* who is outside of us. Second, our imitation of others forms our social identity and gives us language. And third, these two realities form our entire consciousness, personhood, and are the basis of all our human relationships.[6] Indeed, "we are members of one another." Alison concludes, "This means that there is no 'real me' at the

---

6. Alison, *The Joy of Being Wrong*, 28–29.

bottom of it all, when I've scraped away all the things I've learned, all the influences I've undergone."[7]

Verse 26 introduces the issue of anger having a purpose other than sin. Let us place the issue of anger into the framework of mimesis. We have already noted Jesus' use of anger in Mark 3:5. It is used for the power of speaking truth and the healing of others. To "sin" is to let anger serve the function of mimetic rivalry and division. Thus verse 26 depicts this as "the sun going down" to indicate the power of darkness. By placing the energy of anger into the service of speaking truth to our neighbor and serving our neighbor we make no room for the *devil*. The word *devil* in biblical Greek is a compound word made up of *dia* for "through" and *bolos* for "casting apart." "Devil"—*diabolos*—is the force of divide and conquer; it is mimetic rivalry, violence, and death. Christ has captured this power and exposed it from the cross. Our Christ identity now places the energy of human anger in service of speaking truth to neighbor and building up one's neighbor. The salvation story is that of Christ turning us from the power of mimetic rivalry (the devil) and empowering us to live out of the diversity of our gifts in service of our new humanity.

> Ephesians 4:30 And do not grieve the Holy Spirit of God, with which you were marked with a seal for the day of redemption. 31 Put away from you all bitterness and wrath and anger and wrangling and slander, together with all malice, 32 and be kind to one another, tenderhearted, forgiving one another, as God in Christ has forgiven you. 5:1 Therefore be imitators of God, as beloved children, 2 and live in love, as Christ loved us and gave himself up for us, a fragrant offering and sacrifice to God.

Verse 30 uses the imperative form of the Greek verb *lupe (lupay)* preceded by the negative "not" in order to emphasize turning from all forms of rivalry that bring *grief* to the Holy Spirit. *Lupe* is pain to mind and body. The text is stating that the body of Christ is the new humanity that we are marked with by a "seal" in our baptism. This verse continues the theme first stated in Ephesians

7. Ibid.

1:13, "In him you also, when you had heard the word of truth, the gospel of your salvation, and had believed in him, were marked with the seal of the promised Holy Spirit." Verse 31 continues by instructing us against all the forms of mimetic rivalry that divide us against our common identity in Christ and the living narrative of the salvation story (the Holy Spirit) that serves our redemption from violence and death. Verse 32 instructs us to live in the power of God's forgiveness—the power that opens our narrative identity as members of one another in Christ. This passage culminates in 5:1 with our being "imitators of God." The word "imitators"—*mimatie*—is in the nominative case as a noun to indicate our main subject matter. It is preceded by the imperative form of the verb "to be"—*ginomai-ginesthe*. Ephesians provides an imperative against mimetic rivalry in verse 30, followed by an imperative for mimesis formed out of Christ's resurrection and the power of God's forgiveness in verses 32 and 5:1. This means that the power of forgiveness that took place in the resurrection of Jesus Christ comes to us to be embodied in us who hear and live out of the salvation story. In turn this living Word empowers us to proclaim and practice the gospel's power of turning our mimetic rivalry into a new common identity with a variety of gifts for the service of one another in Christ.

We find in Ephesians the basis for using *mimesis* as the lens for understanding scripture. Our alienated identity formed by mimetic rivalry is named *diabolos*—devil—that which casts us apart and sets us in opposition to one another. Christ is the power of mimesis that copies an image of God who provides us diversity in gifts, yet holds us together in a common identity formed by life in the living Word—the salvation story. Ephesians confirms Martin Luther's observations that we as humans are *simul justus et pecatur—simultaneously saint and sinner.* We hold both capacities for creativity for life and rivalry that produces violence and death. As the products of our socially formed mimetic narratives we are in need of a story that will always expose our violent rivalry and turn us to creativity and love for one another. Ephesians provides, I believe, the essential recovery of reading scripture from the perspective of human mimesis; that which Girard discovered through his experience as an anthropologist. Verse 5:2 concludes that Christ is an *offering—prosthoran—gift* given to us; a *sacrifice—thusian*, meaning not the idolatry of one killed and hidden as in pagan mythologies, but as the one who has revealed our violence and whose power of love and forgiveness forms a new humanity in Christ.

# 1 Corinthians

11:23 For I received from the Lord what I also handed on to you, that the Lord Jesus on the night when he was betrayed took a loaf of bread, 24 and when he had given thanks, he broke it and said, "This is my body that is for you. Do this in remembrance of me." 25 In the same way he took the cup also, after supper, saying, "This cup is the new covenant in my blood. Do this, as often as you drink it, in remembrance of me." 26 For as often as you eat this bread and drink the cup, you proclaim the Lord's death until he comes.

THE ABOVE PASSAGE IS taken from Paul's first letter to the Corinthians. These words are used in Christian worship as part of the ritual meal in the sacrament known as "Our Lord's Supper," "Communion," and "Eucharist" from the Greek word meaning "to give thanks" (v. 24). Recall the commentary on baptism in Romans 6. In baptism the death of the self of our mimetic rivalry dies so that a new life in Christ can emerge. The Eucharist is the ongoing ritual of the handing over of new life in Christ. It is important to note that originally baptism and Eucharist were celebrated together in the initiation rites of the early church. The Eastern Rite and Greek Orthodox Church have kept these sacraments together in the initiation of infants and adults. Today their unity is being restored throughout the world-wide church.

Paul states that he "received" this ritual meal from the Lord (v. 23). Recall the commentary from John 20 on resurrection. "The Lord" is present in the lives of the disciples who experienced the power of forgiveness in light of the death of Jesus. In the resurrection they discovered Jesus' life from death present in other people. These people handed onto Paul this ritual meal, and he in turn is repeating it in Corinth. Similar texts can be found in Matthew 26:26–29; Mark 14:22–25; and Luke 22:14–20. Matthew, Mark, and Luke place this ritual within the historical context of a Passover meal taking place with Jesus and his disciples on the night of his arrest, prior to his trial and death. The Gospel of John develops a theological theme of Jesus dying on the day of preparation to be "the new Passover "for the salvation of all people (John 19:31, 42).

In his discussion on the meaning of the words accompanying ritual action in a sacrament, George S. Worgul Jr. addresses the function of what he identifies as *root metaphors*. According to Worgul, root metaphors express the social drama that is the very foundation and bond of a community.[1] I note the following root metaphors in this meal. In verse 24 we find the words "given thanks"—from the Greek *eucharistaesas*. Contained in this word is *charis*—grace, which is also part of the word "gift"—*charismaton*. Here we find that this word for thanks is *not* the language used by Jesus at the last supper. There the word used is "blessing"—*eulogayson*—part of the actual Passover prayers. *Eucharist* represents post resurrection language of "giving thanks." Eucharist is giving thanks for the gift of *forgiveness* from the risen Lord. It was forgiveness that opened the disciples to life beyond themselves—life beyond the violence and death of mimetic rivalry.[2] The words "this is my body given for you" and "this cup is the new covenant in my blood" in verses 24 and 25 are not some form of cannibalistic language, but rather they are words confirming that the story of Jesus' life, death, and resurrection is now at the very core of the lives and identity of those who partake of this meal. The sacrament of Our Lord's Supper celebrates our lives as being part of one another in a new humanity because of the central action of salvation taking place through the death and resurrection of Jesus Christ.

The words "after supper" in verse 25 indicate that this sacramental ritual was at the end of a larger community meal, as it was originally part of a sacramental action at the end of a Passover

---

1. Worgul Jr., *From Magic to Metaphor*, 184–5.

2. *Eucharistaesas* is used in John 6:11 as Jesus gives thanks prior to the feeding of the five thousand.

meal of Jesus and his disciples.[3] Historically, as the Christians found themselves being part of the Roman culture under the emperor Constantine, who made Christianity the official religion of the empire, much of the early meaning of this meal was lost. Writing on the Eucharist in our own era, Tad W. Guzie points out that the depth of the personal process of dying to self in living in Christ is lost at the institutional level of the church.[4] At an institutional level the meaning of Eucharist is often lost in the question of "who is in and who is out." Mimetic rivalry and gate keeping are quick to announce themselves to others. It is my sense that a mimetic reading of the scriptures, our lives, and our context is needed in order to bring us to an encounter with the death and resurrection of Jesus Christ in the Eucharist. It is the living Word of the salvation story that makes present the one who reveals our violence and death, and frees and forgives us so that we may live in a new humanity. The Eucharist is a ritual meal to open our lives to our new humanity in Christ. It does so by releasing the work of God's Spirit in us, which I will take up next.

In the fourth century, Gregory of Nyssa said that the Eucharist is intended to "deify" our bodies as we are joined to Christ in the incarnation—God becoming human.[5] Reading verse 26, in light of a mimetic framework, James Alison writes:

> What lies behind the Eucharistic dynamic is the invitation out of idolatry into being. And the Eucharist is the continuous self-giving of the still small voice as a continuous undoing of the whole world of sacrificial violence we inhabit. The undoing works by providing us continuously with the interpretive and linguistic tools to enable us to discover ourselves, beyond all our own violence and all our own cowardice, as being called into being so as to become co-participators in an unimagined creation. This really is the dynamic of moving on, as the fledgling thrown from the nest gradually finds that she

3. Williams, "The Lord's Supper," in Achtemeier, et al, eds., *Harper's Bible Dictionary*, 576.
4. Guzie, *Jesus and the Eucharist*, 142.
5. Gregory of Nyssa in *Christology of the Later Fathers*, 249.

has been given wings, that they work, and they really do bear her up and beyond.[6]

> 1 Corinthians 12:4 Now there are varieties of gifts, but the same Spirit; 5 and there are varieties of services, but the same Lord; 6 and there are varieties of activities, but it is the same God who activates all of them in everyone. 7 To each is given the manifestation of the Spirit for the common good.

Here we find a construct in Paul that provides us insight into the dynamics of the Spirit of Christ. It precedes the naming of a variety of ministries in 1 Corinthians 12:27–31 that is similar to what we have read in Ephesians 4:11–13. Paul also lists these ministries in Romans 12:6–8. I am focusing on this passage to note that the word "varieties" in verse 4, is from the Greek *diairesis*, meaning "through distribution of a variety in the nature of objects or events."[7] Recall that the word for "devil"—*diabolos*—means "through casting apart" (Ephesians 4:26). The Spirit of Christ is unlike the devil, *diabolos,* that "casts us apart" and places us into divide and conquer mode. The Spirit of Christ divides us for the sake of diversity in our gifts, services, and activities (vs. 5–6). Yet, it is the same Spirit, the same God activating them in everyone.

Jean-Pierre Dupuy points out that what drives human violence in mimetic rivalry is the lack of space due to the loss of a common concern between people. Dupuy writes:

> Resentment, the ultimate evil, occurs when nothing any longer comes between human beings, when no concern for the world, no interest in the world, prevents them from falling over each other. In the absence of an intermediary, rivals are bound to clash with one another in a free-for-all violence, having lost all idea of their own individual interests, to say nothing of a common interest.[8]

---

6. Alison, *Faith Beyond Resentment*, 123.
7. Bauer, *A Greek-English Lexicon*, 229.
8. Dupuy, *The Mark of the Sacred*, 168.

## 1 Corinthians

The Spirit of Christ brings us a diversity of individual gifts and interests. The Spirit of Christ provides differentiation that separates us into space that frees us from mimetic resentment over our being too much alike. Recall our reading of Isaiah 11:1-9. The prophet Isaiah mentioned the coming of the Lord's Spirit in a variety of forms: wisdom, understanding, counsel, might, knowledge, and fear-awe of the Lord (Isaiah 11:2). Christ is the coming of the Lord's Spirit in a diversity of gifts that gives us individual forms of creativity to uniquely set us apart. At the same time I cannot emphasize enough that this individual diversity is for the purpose of "the common good" (v. 7). "Common good" is from the Greek word *sumpheron,* meaning "to bring together for the benefit and advantage of others."[9] Paul brings forth the meaning of this word as he uses it again in 1 Corinthians 10:33. Here, the word is translated as "advantage."

> 1 Corinthians 10:33 just as I try to please everyone in everything I do, not seeking my own *advantage,* but that of many, so that they may be saved.

Old Testament scripture scholar Walter Brueggemann has written:

> The great crisis among us is the crisis of "the common good," the sense of community solidarity that binds all in a common destiny—have and have-nots, the rich and the poor. We face a crisis about the common good because there are powerful forces at work among us to resist the common good, to violate community solidarity, and to deny a common destiny.[10]

We live in a world where multinational corporations have grown to the size and power that has proven to be in conflict with democracy. The 2010 U.S. Supreme Court ruling of Citizens United versus The Federal Election Committee made free speech into money and defined corporations as individuals. As a result, unlimited money now flows into the political process, drowning

---

9. Bauer, *A Greek-English Lexicon,* 960.
10. Brueggemann, *Journey to the Common Good,* 1.

out the representation of individual citizens, corrupting the entire system with the influence of concentrated wealth. The creative diversity we are called to be in Christ is being oppressed by an elite minority with incredible wealth and power who monopolize economic influence to serve their greed. Yet as we have noted from the beginning, this power is blind to its own destruction. Without a diversity of gifts, democracy and freedom are dead and in need of resurrection. It is the salvation story, the gospel in light of this blind mimetic rivalry that restores the diversity of gifts in us needed for the common good.

The paradox at the center of the gospel is that the mimetic energy that makes us part of one another, which sets us in violent conflict and death, is also that which, when revealed to us on the cross of Jesus Christ, can be forgiven and turned into a variety of life-giving gifts for the common good. The Spirit of Christ is the common source who "activates" these diverse gifts in everyone (v. 6). "Activates" is from the Greek word *energon* (energy-works). The Spirit of Christ is able to do this work because it awakens in us a common identity for the common good. The Spirit of Christ awakens us to the reality that for the life that is in us to continue we can only ultimately use our gifts for the benefit of all others, for they are our very future and life. This Christ is our source of the peace that we find in Philippians 4:7, "And *the peace of God, which surpasses all understanding, will guard your hearts and your minds in Christ Jesus.*"

# Romans 1–2

I ADDRESS ROMANS 1–2 within the context of the politics of sexuality in Roman culture at the time Paul is writing his letter to the Romans. This is a passage that is often cited out of its literary context today by those who are anti-gay and anti-LGBT. The continuation of Paul's argumentation in chapter 1 finds its outcome in chapter 2.[1] Following is the text and commentary that follows Paul's argument to its conclusion by re-joining the modern day edited chapters one and two in his letter to the Romans.

> 1:16 For I am not ashamed of the gospel; it is the power of God for salvation to everyone who has faith, to the Jew first and also to the Greek. 17 For in it the righteousness of God is revealed through faith for faith; as it is written, "The one who is righteous will live by faith."

Paul was an overly devout, zealous Jew who embraced the salvation story of his people only to learn that God's salvation included the rest of the world—"everyone who has faith." Paul writes to the Greek-speaking cities and provinces such as Corinth, Thessalonica, and Galatia. "Faith" and "righteousness" are held together as the two identification markers of salvation. In our modern day context, the word "righteousness" often sounds like "self-righteousness." In Greek, the word for righteousness is *dikisunay*—social justice. Paul is about to do justice to the politics of human sexuality by playing upon the hot topic of his time—homosexuality and lesbianism.

---

1. Based on James Alison, "'But the Bible Says . . . '? A Catholic Reading of Romans 1," - Speech given at Mount Saint Agnes Theological Center for Women, Baltimore, January 12, 2004.

The backdrop of the Greek culture that preceded the Romans gives us the context for the start of Paul's case that he is presenting. In her work on the sexual culture of ancient Greece, Marilyn Skinner writes:

> ... our modern dichotomy of "homosexual" and "heterosexual" did not exist for them, and fear of women's aberrant sexual behavior was concentrated upon premarital or adulterous heterosexual relations which threatened the integrity of the community by disrupting lines of descent and inheritance. Sexual practices that could have no reproductive consequences perhaps flew beneath the radar screen.[2]

If homosexuality and lesbianism were mainly beneath the radar screen in Greek culture, why was Paul placing them front and center at the start of his letter to people in Rome? In his work on the history of sexuality, Michael Foucault points out that at the time of Rome there was a rising mistrust of human sexual pleasures in relationship to the self within the hierarchy of Roman culture. The first two centuries of Rome were influenced by the writings of Soranus and Rufus of Ephesus.[3] Plutarch, Epictetus, and Marcus Aurelius wrote on the hazards of sexual pleasure. Self-respect was defined as depriving oneself of pleasure which was confined to procreation and marriage.[4]

Thus Paul plays upon this context because it is on the mind of his audience. Yet, keep in mind the craftiness of Paul and his sense for human mimesis and rivalry. For the following passage can not only be stated regarding the Greeks, but also the Jews. Recall all the sexual practices of the Jews at the time of the prophets.

> 1:18 For the wrath of God is revealed from heaven against all ungodliness and wickedness of those who by their wickedness suppress the truth. 19 For what can be known about God is plain to them, because God has shown it to them. 20 Ever since the creation of the world

2. Skinner, *Sexuality*, 77.
3. Foucault, *The Care of the Self*, 39.
4. Ibid., 41.

his eternal power and divine nature, invisible though they are, have been understood and seen through the things he has made. So they are without excuse; 21 for though they knew God, they did not honor him as God or give thanks to him, but they became futile in their thinking and their senseless minds were darkened. 22 Claiming to be wise, they became fools; 23 and they exchanged the glory of the immortal God for images resembling a mortal human being or birds or four-footed animals or reptiles.

James Alison writes on just what is meant by "the wrath of God" (v. 18). God is not violent. Violence is the product of human mimetic rivalry. According to Alison, "wrath of God" is the byproduct of our human systems of "goodness" that are created over and against another group of people. "Wrath of God" is the result of humans striving for goodness without the grace of God. Alison recalls how no one knew this better than Saul the persecutor of Christians who in his conversion became known to us as Paul. Alison writes:

> One of the amazing insights which (Paul) learned as a result of his conversion from "fiercely loyal bulwark of the system of goodness and differences" to "apostle of the new creation emerging in the midst of all differences"—and that is what "apostle to the Gentiles" effectively means—was the way in which belonging to a system of goodness destroys you. It tells you to love your neighbor as yourself, but then it creates a whole class of neighbors who aren't really your neighbors: people who are cursed through not obeying the law, and thus irredeemably different. This means that, with the best will in the world, you find yourself caught in a double bind: you must love, but you must hate in order to love. Because of this you are divided against yourself and find yourself unable to do the good that you know you should do, but find yourself instead doing evil things that you should not do, but which the system of goodness actually drives you to do. In other words, rather than your being a free adherent of

## Salvation Story

a system of goodness, the system of goodness runs you to produce wrath.[5]

Verses 19–21 speak to all the knowledge of the Greek philosophers such as Plato and Aristotle whose works arrive at the belief in God. Yet, their minds were darkened (v. 22) and in their wisdom they were foolish (v. 23). Why? Paul argues that their image for god became that of humans and animals (v. 24). Paul brings up the issue of *idolatry*—the masking of our human power of mimetic rivalry and violence in images that we then use to direct our lives and world. More specifically, Paul sets the scene for the images of what is now viewed as sexual behavior that mixes the animal and human world (not unlike the one Israel's prophets wrote about even earlier than Greece). In Israel's history, sex was interrelated with the worship of pagan gods and goddesses. Their understanding of agricultural production and its success was ritualized in sexual acts as part of religious idolatry. Now for Paul in Rome, sex is viewed with suspicion as undermining the patriarchal power of Rome's ruling families. Paul plays on this context to lead his readers through "the wrath of God" that brought about his own conversion. Paul thus proceeds with images of sexual exchanges that are equally idolatrous.

> 1:24 Therefore God gave them up in the lusts of their hearts to impurity, to the degrading of their bodies among themselves, 25 because they exchanged the truth about God for a lie and worshiped and served the creature rather than the Creator, who is blessed forever! Amen. 26 For this reason God gave them up to degrading passions. Their women exchanged natural intercourse for unnatural, 27 and in the same way also the men, giving up natural intercourse with women, were consumed with passion for one another. Men committed shameless acts with men and received in their own persons the due penalty for their error.

---

5. Alison, *Broken Hearts and New Creations*, 46.

## Romans 1-2

Marilyn Skinner has researched the sexual art that was done on pottery in Greece around the era of 570 to 550 BCE.[6] The sexual art on the pottery served the purpose of instilling eroticism, yet depending on the type of depiction could also be *porneia*—the depicting of whores, those of the unmarried caste—as well as *satire*—making fun of the lower classes. In some scenes a donkey with a human head and erect penis portrays an insatiable appetite for sex.[7] Every form of penetration, oral, anal, and sex between animals and humans is depicted. One can almost picture Paul with such pottery in hand as he pens the above words to the people of Rome.

Paul is utterly playing upon the goodness system rising in the culture of Rome that is now spreading the message that sexual pleasure depraves the human soul and the self. Rome must secure its political power through economic dynasties that need sexuality controlled within marriage in order to transmit its patriarchal rule. Paul's audience has taken the bait. All the images of whoredom, prostitutes, and outrageous satirical sex have been conjured up by Paul for his readers so that they may look down upon such people in ridicule and judgment. Having set the stage for the "self-righteous" indulgence of the reader, Paul now shifts his focus to an array of human discord and violence that all people partake of as part of their common human mimetic condition. After doing so, Paul reminds them that they cannot stand in judgment of these people, for they are just like them!

> 1:28 And since they did not see fit to acknowledge God, God gave them up to a debased mind and to things that should not be done. 29 They were filled with every kind of wickedness, evil, covetousness, malice. Full of envy, murder, strife, deceit, craftiness, they are gossips, 30 slanderers, God-haters, insolent, haughty, boastful, inventors of evil, rebellious toward parents, 31 foolish, faithless, heartless, ruthless. 32 They know God's decree, that those who practice such things deserve to die—yet

---

6. Skinner, *Sexuality in Greek and Roman Culture*, 77–111.
7. Ibid., 82–83.

they not only do them but even applaud others who practice them.

2:1 Therefore you have no excuse, whoever you are, when you judge others; for in passing judgment on another you condemn yourself, because you, the judge, are doing the very same things. 2 You say, "We know that God's judgment on those who do such things is in accordance with truth." 3 Do you imagine, whoever you are, that when you judge those who do such things and yet do them yourself, you will escape the judgment of God? 4 Or do you despise the riches of his kindness and forbearance and patience? Do you not realize that God's kindness is meant to lead you to repentance? 5 But by your hard and impenitent heart you are storing up wrath for yourself on the day of wrath, when God's righteous judgment will be revealed. 6 For he will repay according to each one's deeds: 7 to those who by patiently doing good seek for glory and honor and immortality, he will give eternal life; 8 while for those who are self-seeking and who obey not the truth but wickedness, there will be wrath and fury. 9 There will be anguish and distress for everyone who does evil, the Jew first and also the Greek, 10 but glory and honor and peace for everyone who does good, the Jew first and also the Greek. 11 For God shows no partiality.

Paul speaks of the people being given up to a "debased mind" (v. 28). The Greek word for "debased" is *adokimon*—unqualified, worthless, base.[8] Yet in the following verses we find Paul listing off all the forms of human behavior and violence that were found in the mainstream of Rome's culture. In the midst of its quest for a purer sexual self, Rome held gladiator violence in its coliseums that combined sex, violence, and death to entertain its citizens. Skinner writes of the psychological dynamic of the audience in the coliseum as "always being on the winning side." This represented the collective order of Rome's patriarchal power over nature and all "others."[9] In verse 32, Paul uses words that allude to this culture

---

8. Bauer, *A Greek-English Lexicon*, 21.
9. Skinner, *Sexuality in Greek and Roman Culture*, 208–11.

with "deserving to die," and the crowd's "applause." Having demonstrated that those who look in judgment upon the sexual misfits of their day are no different from them in terms of mimetic rivalry and violence, Paul lifts the blinders from their eyes in 2:1, by saying that they are in no position to judge, for they are just like these "others."

In verses 2 and 3 Paul addresses the inability of his readers to place themselves into the position of God's judgment. In their mimetic rivalry they are blind to their own harm and violence. In verse 4, Paul turns the image of God from that of judgment to kindness and mercy (grace). Mimetic rivalry renders a false image of God that is the human projection of violence. Here, Paul is firmly addressing the idolatry of Rome's culture that made the "self" into a violent god whose entertainment was the death of those that are "other." The true God is the one who comes with patient mercy for all people, whose "kindness" is meant for "repentance"—*metanoia*—the changing of one's heart and mind.

In verse 5, Paul returns to the theme he began with: "wrath." Note how now it is no longer "God's wrath" that has been revealed. Paul has revealed "wrath" as the violent power of idolatry rooted in the self. God's judgment is yet to be revealed as something entirely other than wrath. In verse 7, Paul applauds those who patiently work for Christ—everyone—the common good, providing honor and dignity to all others—eternal life. In verse 8, Paul admonishes those who follow the latest cultural trend of the self, the way of idolatry. For this way results in the system of goodness and human judgment that brings about the wrath of violence and death. In verses 9 and 10, Paul concludes that both Jew and Greek are joined in this predicament of human idolatry and its wrath. It is God's kindness and mercy that are the source of salvation from this idolatry.

Paul has introduced us to the central theme of his letter to the Romans—the righteousness of God—by enticing us with the subject matter of sexual orientation within the Greco-Roman world's view that those outside of marriage and chastity are the scapegoats of society. Faith in the salvation of God is not by means of the idolatrous power of the self. The "righteousness of God" is founded in social justice grounded in God's grace toward all people. The righteousness of God is actually in opposition to the wrath of god-human rivalry and violence based on self-righteousness. God's righteousness—*dikisunay*—is formed from the same Greek word for justification—*dikaioumenoi*—justice, equitableness, fairness.[10] Justification is the central thesis of Paul's letter to the Romans.

> Romans 3:24: They are now justified by his grace as a gift, through the redemption that is in Christ Jesus.

In his work on justification, Carl Braaten states that "justification is always prior to faith."[11] "Faith is simply the acceptance of one's acceptance . . . The fact that God accepts us as we are."[12] This acceptance of people with differing sexual orientations continues to be a source of division and hate in American culture. This speaks to the confusion between what is determined by the mimetic and what is determined by genetics. We find that a thorough reading of Romans 1 and 2 does not support the judgment of those whose sexual orientation is other than heterosexual. We find that exclusion of "the other" is the work of mimetic rivalry, the human wrath that God's mercy comes to dispel. We need to look to genetics as the source for understanding the variances in human sexual orientation. I believe the wager of James Alison, who argues that LGBT sexual orientation is really part of a minority variant in our human development shared by all populations of the world. Alison writes:

> What is beginning to become apparent is that there is a more or less regular minority of people of both sexes who, entirely independent of circumstance, war, long journeys, imprisonment, cults and so on, simply are principally attracted to people of their sex at an emotional and erotic level. It is furthermore becoming clear that this is in most cases a stable and lifelong feature of who the person is, is not in any sense a dysfunction and

---

10. Bauer, *A Greek-English Lexicon*, 247.
11. Braaten, *Justification*, 42.
12. Ibid.

does not in any way diminish the viability of the person who just is this way. And it is even beginning to become clear that such people are able to develop and receive that full-heartedness of love for each other, that delicate birth of a being—taken out of themselves for the other, the other which is not just for lust, nor a defect of some other sort of love which they really ought to have, but don't seem able to, but is quite simply the real thing, which, when present, is recognized as a gift from and an access to God.[13]

Paul concludes in 2:11 that God shows no partiality. God's righteousness comes freely to all who accept forgiveness for the human rivalries they are in. This is the peace (v. 10) that comes when we are set free from the wrath of our own self-righteousness. The "others" we have judged and persecuted can now be who they are, for we do not have to play the game of our being better than them. God's grace gives us the ability to accept who we are, no longer dependent on a created underclass or scapegoat for our identity. Set free from the wrath of our own mimetic rivalry, we can now live and work for the common good of all others.

---

13. Alison, *Is it Ethical to be Catholic?*

# Epilogue

EVOLUTION LEAVES OUR HUMANITY blind on two accounts; first, we cannot see the schemes of oppression and violence that destroy life to construct our present centralized powers of social order; and second, we are blind to our shared identity that is constructed out of the narratives of our lives. I find René Girard's use of mimetic theory as a key insight to leading us out of our evolutionary blindness. His reading of scripture from the perspective of mimetic theory moves us beyond the reading of these texts as mythology and religion, both of which function to hide human murder. And yet Girard's mimetic theory does more as it also opens us to the discovery of our human identity as a narrative grounded in the life of all others who are part of our being.

In his book *Scripture and the Authority of God: How to Read the Bible Today*, N.T. Wright calls for biblical scholarship to explore new ways.[1] Roman Catholic theologian Karl Rahner once called for the church to:

> ... march valiantly toward the new and not yet experienced, to the outer limits, there where Christian doctrine and conscience can travel no further. In the practical life of the Church today, the only fitting theology is a daring theology... What is certain in this day and age is not the past but the future.[2]

But is the church responding? According to the Pew Research Center, the fastest growing group is the Religious Nones, those who claim no identity with an organized religious body. "One-fifth of the U.S. public and a third of adults under 30—are religiously

---

1. Wright, *Scripture and The Authority of God*, 135.
2. Boff, *Church: Charism and Power*, 58.

# Epilogue

unaffiliated today, the highest percentage ever in Pew Research Center Polling."[3]

Dietrich Bonhoeffer concluded that the church exists only insofar as it exists for others.[4] At the same time Bonhoeffer struggled to imagine a "religionless Christianity," as he sensed that the culture of religion was all too much like that of mythology.[5] Bonhoeffer writes:

> The decisive factor is said to be that in Christianity the hope of the resurrection is proclaimed, and that that means the emergence of a genuine religion of redemption, the main emphasis now being on the far side of the boundary drawn by death. But it seems to me that this is just where the mistake and the danger lie. Redemption now means redemption from cares, distress, fears, and longings, from sin and death, in a better world beyond the grave. But is this really the essential character of the proclamation of Christ in the gospels and by Paul? I should say it is not. The difference between Christian hope of resurrection and the mythological hope is that the former sends (one) back to (their) life on earth in a wholly new way which is even more sharply defined than it was in the Old Testament.
>
> The Christian, unlike the devotees of the redemption myths, has no last line of escape available from earthly tasks and difficulties into the eternal, but, like Christ himself ("My God, why hast thou forsaken me?"), (they) must drink the earthly cup to the lees, and only in doing so is the crucified and risen Lord with (them), and (they) crucified and risen with Christ. This world must not be prematurely written off; in this the Old and New Testaments are one. Redemption myths arise from human boundary-experiences, but Christ takes hold of (one) at the centre of (their) life.[6]

---

3. Pew Research Center, *'Nones' on the Rise*.
4. Bonhoeffer, *Letters and Papers*, 211.
5. Ibid., 153–86.
6. Ibid., 186.

I propose that Girard's contribution of a mimetic reading of scripture is what takes hold of us at our center and leads us beyond religion and mythology and points us toward the living God whose Word is the narrative of salvation from our own destruction. James Fowler identifies the stages of faith development moving from the primal all the way to the universal, yet in reality most of our culture's development is arrested in either the mythic/literal or conventional stages of faith.[7] Why is this? It is because culturally our institutions, including the church, function mainly around the model of centralized power whose very life depends on the continuation of myth/power/violence. It is precisely the breaking out of this model, I believe, that Phyllis Tickle was writing about in her book *The Great Emergence: How Christianity Is Changing and Why*. Tickle writes:

> What is not so easy to discern just yet is how the Great Emergence will interface with the results and consequences of such realignments; and more than any other of North America's Christians, it is emergents themselves who are going to have to reconsider Emergence Christianity. They must begin now to think with intention about what this new form of faith is and is to become; because what once was an engaging but innocuous phenomenon no longer is. The cub has grown into the young lion; and now is the hour of his roaring.[8]

Old Testament scholar Walter Brueggemann maintains that what people are looking for is "not new doctrine or new morality, but new world, new self, new future."[9] The question, according to Brueggemann is whether or not we will allow the biblical texts to "fund our counterimagination."[10] I say that without addressing mimesis—the evolutionary universal basis of our human nature—we will not find our way out of religion, mythology, and the power of our own destructiveness. It is our mimetic human nature that is

---

7. Fowler, "Faith and the Structuring of Meaning," 15–42.
8. Tickle, *The Great Emergence*, 151.
9. Brueggemann, *Texts Under Negotiation*, 25.
10. Ibid.

being redeemed in "the salvation story." Yet this story is living and not merely on the pages of scripture; scripture is but the source that trains our eyes, hearts, and minds "to see" beyond religion, myth, and the cultural narratives that blind us.

In his 2009 book, *The Empathic Civilization: The Race to Global Consciousness*, Jeremy Rifkin envisions a new civilization designed around the decentralized power of green energy. Rifkin sees the development of human empathy as the key factor moving humanity into this new civilization. Yet just two years later in his 2011 book, *The Third Industrial Revolution: How Lateral Power is Transforming Energy, the Economy, and the World*, Rifkin writes:

> There is no inevitability to the human sojourn. History is riddled with examples of great societies that collapsed, promising social experiments that withered, and visions of the future that never saw the light of day. This time, however, the situation is different. The stakes are higher. The possibility of utter extinction is not something the human race ever had to consider before the past half century. The prospect of proliferation of weapons of mass destruction, coupled now with the looming climate crisis, has tipped the odds dangerously in favor of an endgame, not only for civilization as we know it, but for our species.
>
> The Third Industrial Revolution is not a panacea that will instantly cure the ills of society or a utopia that will bring us to the Promised Land. It is, however, a no-frills, pragmatic economic plan that might carry us through to a sustainable post-carbon era. If there is a plan b, I have yet to hear it.[11]

Rifkin notes how special interest groups financed by big oil influence the political process and spread skepticism of climate change in the media.[12] What strikes me about Rifkin's work, especially in the 616 pages of *The Empathic Civilization*, is that he gives no attention to mimetic theory and Girard. Girard is utterly missing from his work. While Rifkin sees the profound rearrang-

11. Rifkin, *The Third Industrial Revolution*, 71–72.
12. Ibid., 158–159.

ing of social relationships with green energy and the possibilities of human empathy, he does not see what is driving the counter forces at work against his vision—mimetic rivalry. Girard's disciple Jean-Pierre Dupuy points out that economics now occupies the place of religion, as the nightmare of competition and impersonal technology replaces human encounter.[13] Just as myth/religion functioned to keep us blind to the violent dynamics of mimesis, today economics function to keep us alienated and uninformed about the social repercussions and environmental implications of international trade agreements.

Edwin Friedman made these critical observations on empathy:

> All entities that are destructive to other entities share one major characteristic that is totally unresponsive to empathy: *they are not capable of self-regulation.* This is an absolutely universal rule of life in this galaxy all or . . . ganisms that lack self-regulation will be *perpetually invading the space of their neighbors* . . . organisms that are unable to self-regulate *cannot learn from their experience* . . .[14]

I would argue that it is the function of the mimetic reading of our lives and culture that is needed precisely for the development of a culture to nurture empathy in people. Centralized structures of power in economy, energy, and the military foster competition over scarcity, and drive the blindness of mimetic rivalry, feeding what seems to be an endless cycle of violence and war. Mimesis runs deeper than the issue of empathy and gets at our very identity. It is in the recovery of our shared narrative mimetic identity, I wager, that human empathy will find a place to grow. Yet, Friedman too, omits any treatment of Girard and mimetic theory.

Meanwhile, Richard Dawkins, representing many atheists, argues for "reciprocal altruism" between humans,[15] and provides

---

13. Dupuy, *The Mark of the Sacred*, 173–4.
14. Friedman, *A Failure of Nerve*, 138.
15. Dawkins, *The God Delusion*, 217.

## Epilogue

his own moral list to replace the Ten Commandments.[16] The problem with Dawkins is that he thinks we can be like the rest of the animals he observes that do well at reciprocal altruism. Dawkins, like the other authors I mentioned above, also gives no attention to Girard and the dynamics of mimesis in humans. Lists of rules and commandments are no match for the dynamic narratives of our human nature that find ways to violate rules and laws. As I pointed out in my preface, Dawkins thinks that religion is merely a meme, an idea, when in reality it is the product of the dynamic process of mimesis that calls for the entire retraining of our eyes, hearts, and minds so that they can track the narrative reality of our humanity.

This biblical commentary is but a few limited illustrations of my engagement with texts together with cultural observations of current events to give a contextual life to "the salvation story" for our times. Your own engagements will produce observations beyond the ones I have made. That is why I planted the texts here, so that you may also engage them. It is the engagements of the text with this lens on human mimesis, I believe, that will lead us to read with a new eye these ancient texts, provoking us to engage in entirely new conversations and dialogue. More so, it will lead us to seeing ourselves "as one another" as we discover the narratives of our life and world opened in this process that we share and hold in common.

This work has brought to my mind that scripture is intended for more than preaching and teaching. In particular, the Gospel was used in an ancient small group process and setting known as the *catechumenate*. Here, not only were the scriptures engaged, but the stories of people's lives were simultaneously engaged. Given that mimesis was part of the very vocabulary and writing of Paul, I am convinced that the first Christians were engaging the Gospel in ways that transformed not only how they saw the world, but also transformed their very identities in order to serve a common mission—love, truth, justice,—and above all—*peace*. Can the present church structure ever re-engage such a process, or must this be part of new emerging communities? One thing I am convinced

16. Ibid., 263–4.

of, whichever the case, if the scriptures are going to be a viable resource of *Godly peace* for us they will need to be engaged beyond religion/mythology.

# Bibliography

Achtemeir, Paul et al. *Harper's Bible Dictionary*, San Francisco: Harper, 1985.
Alison, James. *Broken Hearts and New Creations: Imitations of a Great Reversal.* New York: The Continuum International Publishing Group Inc., 2010.
———. *Faith beyond Resentment: Fragments Catholic and Gay.* New York: Crossroad, 2001.
———. *Is it Ethical to be Catholic? Queer Perspectives.* Panel discussion presented February, 2006. www.jamesalison.co.uk/texts/eng27.html
———. *The Joy of Being Wrong: Original Sin through Easter Eyes.* New York: Crossroad, 1998.
———. *Knowing Jesus.* Springfield: Templegate, 1993.
———. *Living in the End Times: The Last Things Re-imagined.* New York: Crossroad, 1996.
Almond, Steve. *Against Football: One Fan's Reluctant Manifesto.* Brooklyn: Melville House, 2014.
Althaus, Paul. *The Theology of Martin Luther.* Philadelphia: Fortress, 1966.
Altizer, Thomas. *The Gospel of Christian Atheism.* Philadelphia: Westminster, 1966.
Armstrong, Karen. *Fields of Blood: Religion and the History of Violence.* New York: Alfred A. Knopf, 2014.
Batto, Bernhard F. *Slaying the Dragon: Mythmaking in the Biblical Tradition.* Louisville: Westminster John Knox, 1992.
Bauer, Walter. *A Greek-English Lexicon of the New Testament and Other Early Christian Literature,* revised and edited by Frederick William Danker, et al. Chicago: The University of Chicago Press, 2000.
Becker, Ernest. *The Denial of Death.* New York: The Free Press, 1973.
Berry, Thomas et al. *Thomas Berry and the New Cosmology.* Mystic, Conn.: Twenty-Third Publications, 1987.
Black, Edwin. *Internal Combustion: How Corporations and Governments Addicted the World to Oil and Derailed the Alternatives.* New York: St. Martin's Press, 2006.
———. *The Transfer Agreement: The Dramatic Story of the Pact between the Third Reich and Jewish Palestine.* New York: Carroll and Graf, 1999.
Blenkinsopp, Joseph. *A History of Prophecy in Israel: From the Settlement in the Land to the Hellenistic Period.* Philadelphia: Westminster, 1983.
———. *The Pentateuch: An Introduction to the First Five Books of the Bible.* New York: Doubleday, 1992.

# Bibliography

Boff, Leonardo. *Church: Charism and Power: Liberation Theology and the Institutional Church.* New York: Crossroad, 1985.

Bonhoeffer, Dietrich. *Letters and Papers from Prison.* New York: Macmillan, 1967.

Braaten, Carl E. *Justification: The Article by which the Church Stands or Falls.* Minneapolis: Fortress, 1990.

Brueggemann, Walter. *Journey to the Common Good.* Louisville: Westminster John Knox, 2010.

———. *The Prophetic Imagination.* Philadelphia: Fortress, 1978.

———. *A Social Reading of the Old Testament: Prophetic Approaches to Israel's Communal Life.* Minneapolis: Fortress, 1994.

———. *Texts under Negotiation: The Bible and Postmodern Imagination.* Minneapolis: Fortress, 1993.

Buechner, Frederick. *Telling the Truth: The Gospel as Tragedy, Comedy and Fairy Tale.* New York: HarperCollins, 1977.

Campbell, Joseph. *Occidental Mythology: The Masks of God.* New York: Viking Penguin, Inc., 1964.

———. *Primitive Mythology: The Masks of God.* New York: Viking Penguin, Inc., 1964.

Cobb, John B. Jr. and Charles Birch. *The Liberation of Life: From the Cell to the Community.* New York: Cambridge University Press, 1981.

Crossan, John Dominic. *In Parables: The Challenge of the Historical Jesus.* San Francisco: Harper and Row, 1973.

———. *The Power of Parable: How Fiction by Jesus Became Fiction about Jesus.* New York: HarperOne, 2012.

Daly, Mary. *Beyond God the Father: Toward a Philosophy of Women's Liberation.* Boston: Beacon, 1973.

Davies, Brian and G. R. Evans. *Anselm of Canterbury: The Major Works.* Oxford: Oxford University Press, 1998.

Dawkins, Richard. *The Blind Watchmaker: Why the Evidence of Evolution Reveals a Universe without Design.* New York: W. W. Norton, 1996.

———. *The Extended Phenotype: The Gene as the Unit of Selection.* San Francisco: W.H. Freeman, 1982.

———. *The God Delusion.* New York: Houghton Mifflin, 2006.

———. *The Selfish Gene.* New York: Oxford University Press, 1989.

Donovan, Vincent J. *The Church in the Midst of Creation.* Maryknoll: Orbis, 1990.

Dupuy, Jean Pierre. *The Mark of the Sacred: Cultural Memory in the Present.* Translated by M. B. Debevoise. Stanford: Stanford University Press, 2013.

Dykstra, Craig and Sharon Parks. *Faith Development and Fowler.* Birmingham: Religious Education Press, 1986.

Eisler, Riane. *The Chalice and the Blade: Our History, Our Future.* San Francisco: Harper and Row, 1987.

# Bibliography

Eliade, Mircea. *The Nature of Religion: The Significance of Religious Myth, Symbolism, and Ritual within Culture.* New York: Harcourt, Brace and World, 1959.

Fiorenza, Elisabeth Schüssler. *Jesus: Miriam's Child, Sophia's Prophet.* New York: Continuum, 1994.

Forde, Gerhard O. *Justification by Faith: A Matter of Death and Life.* Ramsey: Sigler, 1990.

Foucault, Michael. *The Care of the Self: Volume 3 of The History of Sexuality.* Translated by Robert Hurley. New York: Vintage, 1988.

Fowler, James. "Faith and the Structuring of Meaning" in Craig Dykstra and Sharon Parks. *Faith Development and Fowler.* Birmingham: Religious Education Press, 1986.

Friedman, Edwin H. *A Failure of Nerve: Leadership in the Age of the Quick Fix.* New York: Seabury, 2007.

Friere, Paulo. *Pedagogy of the Oppressed, 30th Anniversary edition.* Camden: Bloomsbury Academic, 2000.

Fromm, Eric. *The Anatomy of Human Destructiveness.* New York: Fawcett, 1973.

———. *The Sane Society.* New York: Fawcett Premier, 1955.

———. *To Have Or To Be.* New York: Bantam, 1981.

———. *You Shall Be As Gods: A Radical Interpretation of the Old Testament and Its Tradition.* New York: Fawcett Premier, 1966.

Gimbutas, Maria. *The Gods and Goddesses of Old Europe: 7000 to 3500 BC Myths, Legends, and Cult Images.* Berkeley and Los Angeles: University of California Press, 1974.

Girard, René. *The One by Whom Scandal Comes.* East Lansing: Michigan State University Press, 2014.

———. *The Scapegoat.* Baltimore: John Hopkins University Press, 1986.

———. *Things Hidden Since the Foundation of the World.* Translated by Stephen Bahn and Michael Mettreer. Stanford: Stanford University Press, 1987.

———. *Violence and the Sacred.* Baltimore: John Hopkins University Press, 1972.

Goldstein, Warren. "Take Me Back to the Ball Game (Variations on a Theme)" in Lee Gutkind and Andrew Blauner. *Anatomy of Baseball.* Dallas: Southern Methodist University Press, 2008.

Graves, Robert. *The White Goddess: A Historical Grammar of Poetic Myths.* New York: Farrar, Straus and Giroux, 1966.

Gutkind, Lee and Andrew Blauner. *Anatomy of Baseball.* Dallas: Southern Methodist University Press, 2008.

Guzie, Tad W. *Jesus and the Eucharist.* New York: Paulist, 1974.

Hall, Douglas John. *Waiting for Gospel: An Appeal to the Dispirited Remnants of Protestant Establishment.* Eugene: Cascade, 2012.

Hammond, Guyton B. *Man in Estrangement: Paul Tillich and Erich Fromm Compared.* Nashville: Vanderbilt University Press, 1965.

Hardy, Edward R., ed. "Gregory of Nyssa" in *Christology of the Later Fathers.* Louisville: John Knox, 1995.

# BIBLIOGRAPHY

Heine, Susanne. *Christianity and the Goddesses: Systematic Criticism of a Feminist Theology*. London: SCM Press LTD, 1987.

Heschel, Abraham Joshua. *God in Search of Man: A Philosophy of Judaism*. New York: Farrar, Straus and Giroux, Inc., 1977.

———. *Man is Not Alone: A Philosophy of Religion*. New York: Farrar, Straus and Giroux, Inc., 1979.

———. *The Prophets: Volume 1*. New York: Harper and Row, 1962.

———. *The Prophets: Volume II*. New York: Harper and Row, 1962.

The Holy See. *Encyclical Letter Laudato SI' of the Holy Father Francis on Care for Our Common Home*. V. Global Inequality.

Hooker, Morna D. "The Letter to the Philippians" in *The New Interpreter's Bible, Volume VII*. Nashville: Abingdon, 1996.

Jenkins, Philip. *Laying Down the Sword: Why We Can't Ignore the Bible's Violent Verses*. New York: HarperOne, 2011.

Jewett, Robert. *The Captain America Complex: The Dilemma of Zealous Nationalism*. Santa Fe: Bear and Company, 1984.

Johnson, Elizabeth A. *She Who Is: The Mystery of God in Feminist Theological Discourse*. New York: Crossroad, 1995.

Klein, Naomi. *The Shock Doctrine: The Rise of Disaster Capitalism*. New York: Picador, 2007.

Kruse, Kevin M. *One Nation Under God: How Corporate America Invented Christian America*. New York: Basic Books, 2015.

Lazareth, William H. *Christians in Society: Luther, the Bible, and Social Ethics*. Minneapolis: Fortress, 2001.

Lerner, Gerda. *The Creation of Patriarchy*: (*Women and History*; Volume 1). Oxford: Oxford University Press, 1987.

Luther, Martin. *Luther's Large Catechism*. Minneapolis: Augsburg, 1967.

———. *The Small Catechism*. Minneapolis: Augsburg, 1979.

Lyden, John C. *Film as Religion: Myths, Morals, and Rituals*. New York: New York University Press, 2003.

Mander, Jerry. *Four Arguments for the Elimination of Television*. New York: Quill, 1978.

Matthews, Victor H. and Don C. Benjamin. *Old Testament Parallels: Laws and Stories from the Ancient Near East*. New York: Paulist, 1991.

McFague, Sallie. *Life Abundant: Rethinking Theology and Economy for a Planet in Peril*. Minneapolis: Fortress, 2001.

Mc Larren, Brian D. *A Generous Orthodoxy*. Grand Rapids: Zondervan, 2004.

Merton, Thomas. *Conjectures of a Guilty Bystander*. Garden City: Doubleday, 1966.

———. *Gandhi on Non-Violence: Selected from Mohandas K. Gandhi's Non-Violence in Peace and War*. New York: New Directions, 1965.

Meyer, Robins. *The Underground Church: Reclaiming the Subversive Way of Jesus*. San Francisco: Jossey-Bass, 2012.

Miller, Kenneth R. *Finding Darwin's God: A Scientist's Search for Common Ground between God and Evolution*. New York: Perennial, 1999.

# BIBLIOGRAPHY

Nelson, Willie. *Roll Me Up and Smoke Me When I Die: Musings from the Road.* New York: HarperCollins, 2012.

Nielsen, Kirsten. *There is Hope for a Tree: The Tree as Metaphor in Isaiah. - Journal for the Study of the Old Testament Series.* Worcester: Sheffield Academic Press, Ltd., 1989.

Nouwen, Henri J. *Thomas Merton: Contemplative Critic.* Liguori: Triumph, 1991.

O'Day, Gail R. "The Gospel of John" in *The New Interpreter's Bible: Volume IX.* Nashville: Abingdon, 1995.

Palmer, Parker J. *The Company of Strangers: Christians and the Renewal of America's Public Life.* New York: Crossroad, 1991.

Pannenberg, Wolfhart. *Faith and Reality.* Translated by John Maxwell. Philadelphia: Westminster, 1977.

———. *Systematic Theology: Volume 3.* Translated by Geoffrey W. Bromiley. Grand Rapids: Eerdmans, 1998.

Patai, Raphael. *The Hebrew Goddess.* New York: Avon, 1978.

Perkins, Pheme. "Ephesians," in *The New Interpreter's Bible: Volume XI.* Nashville: Abingdon, 2000.

Pew Research Center. *'Nones' on the Rise*, October 9, 2012, www.pewforum.org/2012/10/09/nones-on-the-rise.

Pinker, Steven. *How the Mind Works.* New York: W.W. Norton, 1997.

Ricœur, Paul. *Essays on Biblical Interpretation.* Philadelphia: Fortress, 1985.

———. *Oneself as Another.* Translated by Kathleen Blamey. Chicago: The University of Chicago Press, 1992.

———. *The Symbolism of Evil.* Boston: Beacon, 1967.

Rifkin, Jeremy. *The Empathic Civilization: The Race to Global Consciousness.* New York: Jeremy P. Tarcher/Penguin, 2009.

———. *The Third Industrial Revolution: How Lateral Power is Transforming Energy, the Economy, and the World.* New York: Palgrave Macmillan, 2011.

Rohr, Richard and Andreas Ebert. *Discovering the Enneagram: An Ancient Tool for a New Spiritual Journey.* New York: Crossroad, 1992.

Rossing, Barbara R. *The Rapture Exposed: The Message of Hope in the Book of Revelation.* Boulder: Westview, 2004.

Ruether, Rosemary Radford. *Liberation Theology: Human Hope Confronts Christian History and American Power.* New York: Paulist, 1972.

Ruether, Rosemary Radford and Herman J. Ruether. *The Wrath of Jonah: The Crisis of Religious Nationalism in the Israeli-Palestinian Conflict.* Minneapolis: Fortress, 2002.

Russell, Letty M. *Human Liberation in a Feminist Perspective - A Theology.* Philadelphia: Westminster, 1974.

Schneiders, Sandra M. *Women and the Word.* New York: Paulist, 1986.

Schwartz, Regina M. *The Curse of Cain: The Violent Legacy of Monotheism.* Chicago: The University of Chicago Press, 1997.

Shea, John. *Stories of God: An Unauthorized Biography.* Chicago: Thomas More, 1978.

# Bibliography

Skinner, Marilyn B. *Sexuality in Greek and Roman Culture*. Malden: Blackwell, 2005.

Smith-Christopher, Daniel L. "The Book of Daniel: An Introduction, Commentary, and Reflections." In *The New Interpreter's Bible, Volume VII*. Nashville: Abingdon, 1996.

Teilhard De Chardin, Pierre. *Christianity and Evolution*. New York: Harcourt Brace Jovanovich, 1971.

———. *Phenomenon of Man*. Evanston: Harper and Row, 1959.

Tickle, Phyllis. *The Great Emergence: How Christianity Is Changing and Why*. Grand Rapids: Baker, 2012.

Tillich, Paul. *The Courage to Be*. Clinton: Colonial, 1972.

———. *The Dynamics of Faith*. New York: Harper and Row, 1957.

Vahanian, Gabriel. *Wait Without Idols*. New York: George Brazilier, Inc., 1964.

Wink, Walter. *The Powers That Be: Theology for a New Millennium*. New York: Galilee, 1998.

Worgul, George S. Jr. *From Magic to Metaphor: A Validation of the Christian Sacraments*. New York: Paulist, 1980.

www.ingramcontent.com/pod-product-compliance
Lightning Source LLC
Chambersburg PA
CBHW072146160426
43197CB00012B/2262